Mediterra
Cookbook w

The Complete Mediterranean
Cookbook for Beginners 2022 (Vol 1)

By WeLoveBooks99

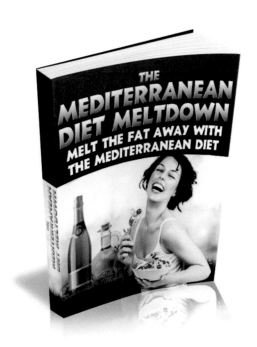

We always love to offer free books to our readers.

Don't forget to get your FREE book below.

https://bit.ly/FreeMediterranean

Table of Contents

What is the Mediterranean Diet?

"Mediterranean diet" is a generic term based on the traditional eating habits in the countries bordering the Mediterranean Sea. There's not one standard Mediterranean diet. At least 16 countries border the Mediterranean. Eating styles vary among these countries and even among regions within each country because of differences in culture, ethnic background, religion, economy, geography and agricultural production. However, there are some common factors.

A Mediterranean-style diet typically includes:

- plenty of fruits, vegetables, bread and other grains, potatoes, beans, nuts and seeds;
- olive oil as a primary fat source;
- dairy products, eggs, fish and poultry in low to moderate amounts.

Fish and poultry are more common than red meat in this diet. It also centers on minimally processed, plant-based foods. Wine may be consumed in low to moderate amounts, usually with meals. Fruit is a common dessert instead of sweets.

Year after year, the Mediterranean diet comes out on top in the U.S. News and World Report annual ranking of best diets. A panel of experts judges various eating plans and popular diets on criteria including how healthy they are, how well they work and how easy they are to follow.

How does Mediterranean Diet work?

Because this is an eating pattern – not a structured diet – you're on your own to figure out how many calories you should eat to lose or maintain your weight, what you'll do to stay active and how you'll shape your Mediterranean menu.

The Mediterranean diet pyramid should help get you started. The pyramid emphasizes eating fruits, veggies, whole grains, beans, nuts, legumes, olive oil and flavorful herbs and spices; fish and seafood at least a couple of times a week; and poultry, eggs, cheese and yogurt in moderation, while saving sweets and red meat for special occasions. Top it off with a splash of red wine (if you want), remember to stay physically active and you're set.

While certainly not required, a glass a day for women and two a day for men is fine if your doctor says so. Red wine contains resveratrol, a compound that seems to add years to life –though you'd have to drink hundreds or thousands of glasses to get enough resveratrol to possibly make a difference.

The Mediterranean diet pyramid was developed based on the eating habits of long-living adults in the Mediterranean. It follows a general food pyramid guideline (not specific quantities) and encourages communal eating and an active lifestyle.

Mediterranean Diet Pyramid

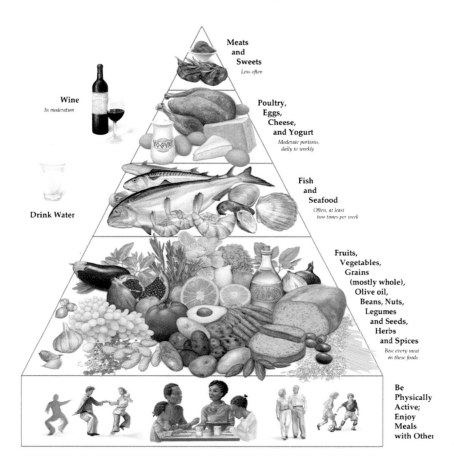

Meats and Sweets
Less often

Wine
In moderation

Poultry, Eggs, Cheese, and Yogurt
Moderate portions, daily to weekly

Fish and Seafood
Often, at least two times per week

Drink Water

Fruits, Vegetables, Grains (mostly whole), Olive oil, Beans, Nuts, Legumes and Seeds, Herbs and Spices
Base every meal on these foods

Be Physically Active; Enjoy Meals with Other

Eggs with Zucchini Noodles

Preparation time:10min / **Cooking time:**15min / **Servings:** 2
Ingredients:
- 3 Zucchini spiralized into noodles
- 2 Tbsp Olive Oil
- 1 Cup Cherry Tomatoes halved
- Sea salt and freshly ground black pepper, to taste
- 4 Eggs
- 1 Avocado halved and thinly sliced
- ¼ Cup Crumbled Feta Cheese
- 1 Tbsp Fresh Chopped Parsley

Directions:
-Preheat the oven to 350°F. Lightly spray a baking sheet with cooking spray.
-In a large bowl, toss the zucchini noodles, cherry tomatoes and olive oil to combine. Season with salt and pepper to your taste.
-Divide into 4 even portions on your baking sheet and shape each into a nest, then gently crack an egg in the center of each one.
-Bake until the eggs are set, 8-12 minutes. Top with avocado slices, crumbled cheese, and parsley. Enjoy!
Nutrition:calories 262kcal;protein 10g;carbs 11g ;fat 21g;fiber 5g ;

Banana Oatmeal

Preparation time:10 minutes / **Servings:** 2
Ingredients:
- 1/2 cup rolled oats
- 1/4 tsp salt
- 1 cup milk of choice
- 1/4 cup water or additional milk of choice
- 1 large very overripe banana, mashed
- optional 1/4 tsp cinnamon
- optional crushed walnuts, mini chocolate chips, shredded coconut, etc.
- sweetener of choice, if needed

Directions:
Combine all ingredients in a small pot. Bring to a boil over medium heat. Once boiling, stir only occasionally to prevent sticking or boiling over. It will eventually thicken. Sweeten as desired. Add your favorite toppings. I like peanut butter, mini chocolate chips, or the healthy nutella recipe linked earlier in this post. Serve hot, or refrigerate overnight and serve either hot or cold the next day.

Nutrition:calories 140kcal ;protein 3.8g ;carbs 55g ; fat 2.5g ;

Peppers Fritata

Preparation time:15min / **Cooking time:**30min / **Servings:** 6
Ingredients:
- 2 medium onions, halved and thinly sliced
- 2 tablespoons olive oil
- 2 garlic cloves, minced
- 1/2 cup chopped roasted sweet red peppers, drained
- 1/2 cup chopped pimiento-stuffed olives
- 3 cups cubed Italian bread
- 1/2 cup crumbled feta cheese
- 6 eggs, lightly beaten
- 1/2 cup chicken broth
- 1/4 teaspoon pepper

Directions:
- In a large skillet, saute onions in oil until tender. Add garlic; cook 1 minute longer. Remove from the heat. Stir in red peppers and olives. Place bread cubes in a greased 9-in. deep-dish pie plate. Top with onion mixture and cheese.
-In a large bowl, whisk the eggs, broth and pepper; pour over cheese. Bake at 375° for 30-35 minutes or until a knife inserted in the center comes out clean. Let stand for 5 minutes before cutting into wedges.

Nutrition:calories 300kcal;protein 35g;carbs8g ;fat 20g;fiber 6g ;

Chickpea Quinoa Bowl

Preparation time:10min / **Cooking time:**10min / **Servings:** 4
Ingredients:
- 1 (7 ounce) jar roasted red peppers, rinsed
- ¼ cup slivered almonds
- 4 tablespoons extra-virgin olive oil, divided
- 1 small clove garlic, minced
- 1 teaspoon paprika
- ½ teaspoon ground cumin
- ¼ teaspoon crushed red pepper (optional
- 2 cups cooked quinoa
- ¼ cup Kalamata olives, chopped
- ¼ cup finely chopped red onio
- 1 (15 ounce) can chickpeas, rinsed
- 1 cup diced cucumber
- ¼ cup crumbled feta cheese
- 2 tablespoons finely chopped fresh parsley

Directions:
-Place peppers, almonds, 2 tablespoons oil, garlic, paprika, cumin and crushed red pepper (if using) in a mini food processor. Puree until fairly smooth.
-Combine quinoa, olives, red onion and the remaining 2 tablespoons oil in a medium bowl.
- To serve, divide the quinoa mixture among 4 bowls and top with equal amounts of the chickpeas, cucumber and the red pepper sauce. Sprinkle with feta and parsley.

Nutrition:calories 480kcal ;protein 12g ;carbs 48g ;fat 24g ;fiber 8g

Avocado Apple Smoothie

Preparation time: 5min / **Cooking time:** 0min / **Servings:** 2
Ingredients:
- 1 ripe avocado, peeled, pitted and cubed
- 2 small apples, cored and diced
- 2 cups milk
- 1 cup cold water or ice cubes
- 1/2 overripe banana
- 2 tablespoons fresh lemon, lime, or orange juice

Directions:
-Put all the ingredients in the blender.
-Put the top on tightly. Turn on the blender to medium speed and blend until the mixture is smooth, 30-60 seconds.
-Divide the smoothie equally between 2 glasses and serve right away or cover and refrigerate up to 1 hour

Nutrition:calories 165kcal ; carbs 21g ; fat 10g ; fiber 6g ;

Avocado Toast

Preparation time: 5 min / **Cooking time:** 2 min / **Servings:** 2
Ingredients:
- 1 slice of bread (I like thick-sliced whole-grain bread best)
- ½ ripe avocado
- Pinch of salt
- Optional: Any of the extra toppings suggested in this post

Directions:
-Toast your slice of bread until golden and firm.
-Remove the pit from your avocado. Use a big spoon to scoop out the flesh. Put it in a bowl and mash it up with a fork until it's as smooth as you like it. Mix in a pinch of salt (about ⅛ teaspoon) and add more to taste, if desired.
-Spread avocado on top of your toast. Enjoy as-is or top with any extras offered in this post (I highly recommend a light sprinkle of flaky sea salt, if you have it).

Nutrition:calories 237kcal ;protein 6g ;carbs 21g ; fat 15.8g ; fiber 8g ;

Mini Frittatas with Spinach and Red Pepper

Preparation time: 10min / **Cooking time:** 22min / **Servings:**12
Ingredients:
- 1 teaspoon olive oil
- 1/2 red bell pepper, diced small (about 1/2 cup)
- 1/2 small yellow onion, diced small (about 1/2 cup)
- about 3 cups loosely packed spinach, roughly chopped
- 4 eggs
- 4 egg whites
- 1/4 cup skim milk
- 2/3 cup shredded sharp cheddar cheese
- salt and pepper to taste

Directions:
-Preheat oven to 375°F. Grease or spray a tin for 12 muffins.
-In a medium frying pan, heat the oil over medium high heat. When hot, add peppers and onions and saute until softened, about five minutes, stirring occasionally. Add spinach and stir gently until wilted. Remove from heat.
-Meanwhile, in a large bowl, whisk together eggs, egg whites, skim milk, cheese, salt and pepper.
-Pour egg mixture into prepared muffin tin so that each one is about 1/2 to 2/3 full. Add sauteed vegetables evenly to each of the 12 muffins.
-Bake for 20-25 minutes or until puffed up and golden brown. Leave in muffin tin for about 5 minutes before removing and serving.

Nutrition: 1 mini frittatas: calories 100kcal ;protein 8g ;carbs 3g ; fat 6g ; fiber 1g ;

Mixed Berry Oatmeal

Preparation time: 1 min / **Cooking time:** 5 min / **Servings:** 2
Ingredients:
- 1 cup Bob's Red Mill Quick Cooking Rolled Oats
- 1 cup mixed berries - blueberries, strawberries, blackberries, whatever you wish
- 1 tbsp honey
- 2 tsp brown sugar, divided

Directions:
-Cook the oats according to package directions.
-While the oats are cooking, combine the berries and honey in a saucepan set over medium heat on the stove. Cook until the fruit releases its juices -- about 3-5 minutes. Remove from heat.
-Divide the oatmeal between two bowls. Top each with 1 teaspoon of brown sugar, and 1/2 of the berry mixture.
-Enjoy!

Nutrition:calories 248kcal ;protein 6g ;carbs 51g ; fat 3g ;fiber 8g ;

Oatmeal with Sun-dried Tomato and Parmesan Cheese

Preparation time: 7 min / **Cooking time:** 8 min / **Servings:** 2
Ingredients:
- 1 cup, rolled oats
- 2 cups, vegetable or chicken stock
- 2 teaspoons, milled flaxseed
- 1 teaspoon, dried parsley
- 3 slices, sun-dried tomato
- 1/2 tablespoon, olive oil
- grated Parmesan cheese

Directions:
-Boil oatmeal and stock in a pot. Sprinkle in flaxseed. Cook for 8 minutes.
-Add in dried parsley to the cooked oatmeal.
-Finely chop sun-dried tomatoes.
-Serve oatmeal with olive oil, sun-dried tomato pieces, and grated Parmesan cheese.

Nutrition:calories 180kcal ;protein 2g ;carbs 4g ; fat 17g ; fiber 2g;

Quinoa Muffins

Preparation time: 10min / **Cooking time:** 30min / **Servings:**12
Ingredients:
- 1 cup quinoa, rinsed
- 1/4 cup vegetable oil, such as safflower, plus more for pan
- 2 cups all-purpose flour, plus more for pan
- 3/4 cup packed dark-brown sugar
- 1 1/2 teaspoons baking powder
- 1 teaspoon salt
- 1/2 cup raisins
- 3/4 cup whole milk
- 1 large egg
- 1 teaspoon pure vanilla extract

Directions:
-Preheat oven to 350 degrees. In a medium saucepan, bring quinoa and 1 cup water to a boil. Reduce to a simmer; cover, and cook until water has been absorbed and quinoa is tender, 11 to 13 minutes.
-Meanwhile, brush a standard 12-cup muffin pan with oil; dust with flour, tapping out excess. In a medium bowl, whisk together flour, sugar, baking powder, salt, raisins, and 2 cups cooked quinoa; reserve any leftover quinoa for another use.
-In a small bowl, whisk together oil, milk, egg, and vanilla. Add milk mixture to flour mixture, and stir just until combined; divide batter among prepared muffin cups.
-Bake until toothpick inserted into the center of a muffin comes out clean, 25 to 30 minutes. Cool muffins in pan, 5 minutes; transfer to a wire rack to cool completely.
Nutrition:calories 120kcal ;protein 7g ;carbs 10g ; fat 5g ; fiber 1g;

Quinoa with Eggs and Vegetables

Preparation time: 10min / **Cooking time:** 15min / **Servings:** 2
Ingredients:
- 1 medium bell pepper red, yellow, or orange
- 1 medium carrot
- 1 jalapeno pepper
- 1 tbsp grapeseed oil or other kind
- 2 tbsp soy sauce
- 3 eggs
- 2 cups cooked quinoa
- ¼ cup chopped scallion

Directions:
-Prep the vegetables. Cut the peppers into strips. Using a vegetable peeler, shave the carrot into flat strips. Then, dice the jalapeño pepper.
-Place a non-stick skillet over medium-high heat and add the oil and bell pepper. Cook for 3 minutes, until the pepper just starts to soften.
-Add the carrot strips and jalapeño, and then cook for another 2 minutes.
-Add the soy sauce and eggs to the pan and cook until the eggs are almost set. At this point, add the cooked quinoa and cook until heated through.
-Stir in the scallions and serve immediately. Garnish with sliced jalapeno, if desired.

Nutrition:calories 422kcal ;protein 19g ;carbs 48g ; fat 17g ; fiber 8g ;

Stuffed Baked Tomatoes

Preparation time: 15min / **Cooking time:** 30min / **Servings:** 6
Ingredients:
- 6 medium tomatoes
- 1 cup garlic/cheese croutons, crushed
- 2 tablespoons grated Parmesan cheese
- 2 tablespoons grated American or cheddar cheese
- 4 tablespoons melted butter
- 1/2 teaspoon salt
- 1/4 teaspoon freshly ground pepper
- Chopped fresh parsley for garnish

Directions:
-Preheat oven to 350°. Cut a thin slice off the top of each tomato.
Scoop out pulp, leaving a 1/2-in. shell. Invert shells onto paper
towels to drain. Mix stuffing ingredients except parsley; spoon
stuffing into tomatoes. Sprinkle with parsley.
-Place tomatoes in a baking dish; cover with aluminum foil to
prevent over-browning of stuffing. Bake until tomatoes are tender
and stuffing is hot, about 30 minutes.

Nutrition: 1 each: calories 145kcal ;protein 3g ;carbs 12g ; fat 11g ;
fiber 2g ;

Scrambled Eggs

Preparation time: 10min / **Cooking time:** 10min / **Servings:** 2
Ingredients:
- large eggs 4
- milk 1/4 cup
- salt pinch
- pepper pinch
- butter 2 tsp.

Directions:

-BEAT eggs, milk, salt and pepper in medium bowl until blended.

-HEAT butter in large nonstick skillet over medium heat until hot.
POUR in egg mixture. As eggs begin to set, gently PULL the eggs
across the pan with a spatula, forming large soft curds.

-CONTINUE cooking—pulling, lifting and folding eggs—until
thickened and no visible liquid egg remains. Do not stir constantly.
REMOVE from heat. SERVE immediately.

Nutrition:calories 200kcal ;protein 28g ;carbs 4g ; fat 20g ;

Watermelon "Pizza"

Preparation time: 10 min / **Cooking time:** 0min / **Servings:** 12
Ingredients:
- 4 oz cream cheese, softened
- 4 oz cool whip
- 1/4 cup powdered sugar
- 1/2 tsp vanilla
- 2 slices watermelon
- 1/2 cup sliced strawberries
- 1/2 cup sliced peaches
- 1/2 cup sliced kiwi
- 1/2 cup blueberries

Directions:
-Beat the softened cream cheese.
-Mix in the cool whip.
-Stir in the powdered sugar and vanilla.
-Spread 1/2 cup of the cream cheese frosting on each slice of watermelon.
-Top with sliced fruit.

Nutrition: per serving:calories 90kcal ;protein 1g ;carbs 12g ; fat 3g ; fiber 1g ;

Cheese and Ham Muffins

Preparation time: 10min / **Cooking time:** 25min / **Servings:**12
Ingredients:
- 275g plain flour
- 1tbsp baking powder
- 1 tsp caster sugar
- 125g mature cheddar cheese, grated
- 125g cooked ham, chopped
- 7 sundried tomatoes in oil, drained and chopped
- 2tbsp chives, freshly snipped
- 2 medium eggs
- 200ml (7floz) buttermilk or semi-skimmed milk
- 90ml (3½floz) sunflower oil

Directions:
-Preheat the oven to gas 5, 190°C, fan 170°C. Line a muffin tin with 12 paper muffin cases. Sift together the flour and baking powder in a large bowl.
-Mix in the sugar, ½tsp salt, 75g (3oz) cheese, ham, sundried tomatoes and chives.
-In another bowl, beat together the eggs, buttermilk (or milk) and oil and pour over the dry ingredients. Stir until just combined, fill the muffin cases and sprinkle the tops with the remaining cheese. Bake for 20-25mins until risen.

Nutrition: per serving calories: 228kcal

Avocado Chickpea Pizza
Preparation time: 20min / **Cooking time:** 25min / **Servings:** 4
Ingredients:
- 1 batch of gluten-free pizza crust (or crust of choice)
- 2 tbsp olive oil or any other oil (divided)
- 1/2 cup tomato sauce (tomato passata)
- 4 tbsp coconut milk canned (or any other plant-based milk)
- 1 tbsp balsamic vinegar (or apple cider vinegar)
- 1 tbsp hot sauce (or more/less to taste)
- 1 tsp coconut sugar (or regular sugar)
- spice mix (1 tsp each of smoked paprika, onion powder, garlic powder)
- sea salt and pepper to taste
- 1 batch of easy vegan cheese sauce
- 1 avocado
- 1 15 oz can chickpeas

Directions:
-Make the pizza crust as per the instructions in the recipe. Preheat oven to 200 degrees C (390 degrees F).
-To make the sauce, mix 1 tbsp oil and all other sauce ingredients in a bowl with a whisk. Spread the sauce (but save 3-4 tbsp) on the pizza crust and put the pizza in the oven for 10 minutes.
-Heat 1 tbsp oil in a skillet, add the remaining 3-4 tbsp of sauce and the chickpeas and fry for 3-5 minutes over medium heat.
-Spread the chickpea mixture and the vegan cheese sauce onto the pizza and put it back into the oven for another 10-15 minutes (or until crispy).
-Peel the avocado, remove the stem, and cut it into pieces and put it on the pizza right before serving. Season again with sea salt/pepper/spices if desired. Enjoy your delicious avocado chickpea pizza!
Nutrition:calories 188kcal ;protein 2g ;carbs 8g ; fat 32g ; fiber 4g;

Quinoa with Blueberries and Bananas

Preparation time: 10min / **Cooking time:** 30min / **Servings:** 4
Ingredients:
- 1 cup water
- 1–1/2 cups milk (cow, almond or coconut)
- 1 teaspoon pure vanilla extract
- 3 tablespoons brown sugar
- 1/4 teaspoon ground cinnamon
- 1 cup quinoa, rinsed well
- Toppings:blueberries;banana slices;nuts; milk (cow, almond or coconut); drizzle of honey or maple syrup

Directions:
-In a medium, heavy bottom saucepan, combine the water, 1-1/2 cups milk, vanilla, quinoa, and salt. Bring to a boil over medium-high heat; stirring occasionally. Reduce heat to low; cover with a vented lid and simmer for 15 minutes. Stir occasionally as needed.
-Stir in the brown sugar and cinnamon. Cover again with a vented lid and cook for another 5 minutes or until most of the liquid has absorbed. Stir as needed. Spoon the quinoa into bowls, top with milk, blueberries, banana slices, nuts and a drizzle of honey or maple syrup if desired.

Nutrition: calories 265kcal

Spiced Chickpea Bowls

Preparation time: 10min / **Cooking time:** 20min / **Servings:** 6
Ingredients:
- 1 tablespoon olive oil
- 1/4 cup chopped onion
- 1 clove garlic, minced
- 1 tablespoon each – chili powder and cumin
- 1 teaspoon each – turmeric and garam masala
- 1 teaspoon sea salt
- dash of each -cinnamon and cayenne (to taste)
- 2 14–ounce cans chickpeas
- 2 14–ounce cans fire roasted diced tomatoes

Directions:
-Heat the olive oil in a large skillet over medium heat. Add the onion; saute until soft. Add the garlic, spices, salt, and chickpeas – stir until very fragrant. Add the tomatoes (undrained) and simmer for 20 minutes while you prep the other ingredients.
-Chop the cucumber, cook the couscous, and mince the herbs. Arrange bowls with desired amounts of all ingredients. Voila!

Nutrition:calories 181kcal ;protein 6g ;carbs 27g ; fat 6g ; fiber 8g;

Avocado Spread

Preparation time: 5 min / **Cooking time:** 0 min / **Servings:** 1
Ingredients:

- 2 Medium Ripe Avocados
- ¼ teaspoon Salt
- Black Pepper , a generous pinch
- ½ Lemon , juice only, see note 1
- 2 tablespoons Extra Virgin Olive Oil , see note 2
- 1 tablespoon Chia Seeds , see note 3
- Chili Peppers , to taste, see note 4

Directions:

-Half the avocados and remove pits. Take out the flesh and transfer it into a bowl. Mash it until smooth (or to you liking). Add salt, pepper, lemon juice, olive oil, chia seeds and stir well.

-Taste it and season, if needed. Finely chop chili and either stir it into the spread or just sprinkle some over.

Nutrition:calories 60kcal ;protein 1g ;carbs 3g ; fat 6g ; fiber 2g ;

Cheesy Yogurt

Preparation time: 4 hours / **Cooking time:** 0 min / **Servings:** 4
Ingredients:
- 1 cup Greek yogurt
- 1 tablespoon honey
- ½ feta cheese crumbled

Directions:
- In a blender, combine the yogurt with the honey and the cheese and pulse well.
- Divide into bowls and freeze for 4 hours before serving for breakfast.

Nutrition: calories 161kcal ;protein 6g ;carbs 11g ; fat 10g ; fiber 0g ;

Baked Omelet

Preparation time: 15min / **Cooking time:** 40min / **Servings:** 4
Ingredients:
- 8 eggs
- 1 cup milk
- ½ teaspoon seasoning sal
- 3 ounces cooked ham, diced
- ½ cup shredded Cheddar cheese
- ½ cup shredded mozzarella cheese
- 1 tablespoon dried minced onion

Directions:
-Preheat oven to 350 degrees F (175 degrees C). Grease one 8x8 inch casserole dish and set aside.
-Beat together the eggs and milk. Add seasoning salt, ham, Cheddar cheese, Mozzarella cheese and minced onion. Pour into prepared casserole dish.
-Bake uncovered at 350 degrees F (175 degrees C) for 40 to 45 minutes.

Nutrition: per serving calories 314kcal ;protein 24g ;carbs 6g ; fat 21g ;

Baked Sweet Potato

Preparation time: 5min / **Cooking time:** 55 min / **Servings:** 4
Ingredients:
- 4 sweet potatoes, scrubbed clean
- 4 tbsp. butter
- Kosher salt
- Freshly ground black pepper

Directions:

-Preheat oven to 425°. On a baking sheet lined with aluminum foil, prick sweet potatoes all over with a fork.
-Bake until tender, 45 to 50 minutes.
-Let cool, then split the tops open with a knife and top with a pat of butter.
-Season with salt and pepper before serving.

Nutrition:calories 308kcal ;protein 7g ;carbs 38g ; fat 2g ; fiber 8g ;

Cauliflower Fritters

Preparation time: 10min / **Cooking time:** 15min / **Servings:** 2
Ingredients:
- 5 cups chopped cauliflower florets
- 2 eggs
- ½ cup all purpose flour
- ½ tsp baking powder
- salt and pepper to taste
- vegetable oil for frying

Directions:

-Place the cauliflower into the food processor and process until finely minced.
-Transfer the cauliflower into a large mixing bowl and add the rest of the ingredients, excluding the vegetable oil. Mix everything well. (You should have a nice, paste-like mixture. If the mixture looks a little too soft and moist – add some more flour.)
-Using an ice-cream scoop as a measure, form small, ⅓ inch-thick patties. You can make them smaller or larger depending on your personal preference.
-Fry the patties on medium heat, in a small amount of vegetable oil for about 2 minutes per side.
-Serve the fritters with sour cream or your favorite sauce.

Nutrition: calories 272kcal ;protein 11g ;carbs 57g ; fiber 8g ;

Tuna Salad

Preparation time: 5 min / **Cooking time:** 0 min / **Servings:** 6
Ingredients:
- 4 (5 ounce) cans tuna packed in water drained (see note 1)
- 1 cup mayonnaise or less to taste (see note 2)
- 1/3 cup celery finely chopped (about 1 rib)
- 2 tablespoons red onion minced, about 2 small slices
- 2 tablespoon sweet pickle relish (see note 3)
- 1 tablespoon fresh lemon juice
- 1 clove garlic minced
- salt and freshly ground black pepper

Directions:
-In a medium bowl, combine tuna, mayonnaise, celery, onion, relish, lemon juice, and garlic.

-Season to taste with salt and pepper (I like ½ teaspoons salt and ¼ teaspoon pepper). Serve immediately or cover and chill until serving.

Nutrition:calories 345kcal ;protein 11g ;carbs 3g ; fat 1g ; fiber 1g;

Veggie Quiche

Preparation time: 20min / **Cooking time:** 35min / **Servings:** 1
Ingredients:
- 1 sheet frozen Puff Pastry, thawed
- 6 large eggs
- ½ cup heavy whipping cream
- ¼ cup milk
- -½ teaspoon garlic salt
- ¼ teaspoon black pepper
- ½ teaspoon dried parsley
- ½ teaspoon dried onion flakes
- ¾ cup shredded parmesan cheese
- 1 ½ cup shredded cheddar cheese
- 1 ½ cup chopped fresh vegetables (I used green pepper, red pepper, mushrooms and broccoli)

Directions:
-Allow frozen puff pastry to thaw, according to package directions (about 15 minutes). Once thawed, press into a 9-inch pie plate.
-Beat eggs, heavy cream, milk, garlic, pepper, parsley and onion flakes until fully combined. Add in cheeses and vegetables. Pour into pie plate.
-Bake in a 375 degree oven for 30-35 minutes. Remove and allow to cool 10-15 minutes before slicing and serving. ENJOY.
Nutrition:calories 277kcal ;protein 15g ;carbs 10g ; fat 20g ; fiber 2g ;

Halloumi and Tomato Salad

Preparation time: 10min / **Cooking time:** 5min / **Servings:** 4
Ingredients:
- 2 large tomatoes
- 10 cherry tomatoes
- 250g halloumi
- 3 tbsp extra virgin olive oil, plus extra for brushing
- 1 tbsp red wine vinegar
- 5g mint

Directions:
-Heat the barbecue. Slice the large tomatoes and halve the cherry tomatoes; reserve any juices that are released. Season well.
-Slice the Halloumi into fingers. Oil the grill and cook the cheese on both sides until well marked. Whisk the olive oil and vinegar together with some sea salt and pepper, then whisk in any tomato juices.
-Arrange the tomatoes and Halloumi on a large serving platter. Scatter with mint and drizzle with the dressing.

Nutrition:calories 314kcal ;fat 28g ;

Millet with Zucchini and Chickpeas

Preparation time: 5min / **Cooking time:** 35min / **Servings:** 8
Ingredients:
- 3 tablespoons extra-virgin olive oil, divided
- 2 medium zucchini, diced into 1" cubes
- Salt and Pepper
- 1 large yellow onion, diced
- 4 cloves garlic, minced
- 2 cups millet
- 3 cups low sodium vegetable broth
- 3 cups water
- 1 tsp curry powder
- 1 (15-ounce) can of chickpeas, no salt added, rinsed and drained
- ¾ cup golden raisins (optional)

Directions:
-In a medium-sized pot, heat one tablespoon olive oil on medium heat. Add zucchini with salt and pepper to taste, stirring occasionally. Sauté for 4 to 5 minutes, or until the vegetable softens but retains slight crispness. Remove zucchini from pot and set aside.
-In the same pot, heat two tablespoons olive oil on medium heat. Add onions and garlic, and sauté for 4 to 5 minutes, or until onions are softened and translucent.
-Add the millet to the pot, and toast for 2 to 3 minutes, stirring occasionally.
-Add the vegetable broth, water, and curry powder. Bring to a boil, then simmer on low, covered, for 15 to 20 minutes, checking occasionally.
-When the millet is softened, turn off the heat and allow it to sit for 5 minutes. Fluff with fork, before adding zucchini, chickpeas, and raisins (if using). Season to taste with salt and pepper, and return to heat for 1 to 2 minutes to warm if necessary

Nutrition:calories 370kcal ;protein 10g;carbs 63g ; fat 9g; fiber 9g;

Chicken Salad

Preparation time: 20min / **Cooking time:** 0 min / **Servings:** 6
Ingredients:
- ⅓ cup lemon juice
- 2 tablespoons snipped fresh mint
- 2 tablespoons snipped fresh basil
- 2 tablespoons olive oil
- 1 tablespoon honey
- ¼ teaspoon ground black peppe
- 5 cups shredded romaine lettuce
- 2 cups cut-up cooked chicken breast
- 2 plum tomatoes, cut into wedge
- 1 (15 ounce) can garbanzo beans (chickpeas), rinsed and drained
- 2 tablespoons pitted Kalamata olives, quartered (Optional)
- 2 tablespoons crumbled reduced-fat feta cheese
- 6 Whole kalamata olives for garnish (Optional)

Directions:
- In a screw-top jar, combine lemon juice, mint, basil, olive oil, honey, and black pepper to make dressing. Cover and shake well.
- Place lettuce on a large platter. Top with chicken, tomatoes, garbanzo beans, the quartered olives (if using), and feta cheese. Drizzle with dressing. If desired, garnish individual servings with whole olives.

Nutrition: per serving calories 237kcal ;protein 20g ;carbs 23g ; fat 8g ; fiber 5g ;

Skillet Chicken with Garlic Herb Butter Sauce

Preparation time: 8min / **Cooking time:** 15min / **Servings:** 4
Ingredients:
- 4 (6 oz) boneless, skinless chicken breasts
- 1 1/2 Tbsp minced garlic (4 cloves)
- 1 Tbsp olive oil
- Salt and freshly ground black pepper
- 1/3 cup low-sodium chicken stock or dry white wine
- 4 Tbsp unsalted butter, divided
- 2 tsp chopped fresh sage*
- 1 tsp chopped freshy thyme
- 1 tsp chopped fresh rosemary

Directions:
-Heat a large 12-inch skillet over medium-high heat. Pound thicker parts of chicken with the flat side of a meat mallet to even their thickness.
-Dab chicken dry with paper towels, then season both sides of chicken with salt and pepper. Add oil to skillet, then add chicken.
-Cook chicken about 5 - 6 minutes per side or until center registers 165 degrees on an instant read thermometer. Transfer to a plate.
-Reduce burner temperature slightly, then melt 1 1/2 Tbsp butter in same skillet. Add in garlic and sage and saute until garlic is golden brown, about 30 seconds.
-Pour in chicken broth and scrape up browned bits from bottom of pan. Dice remaining butter into 3 pieces then add to skillet along with thyme and rosemary. Stir until butter is melted.
-Return chicken to pan and spoon sauce over top. Serve warm.

Nutrition:calories 335kcal ;protein 36g ;carbs 1g ; fat 19g ;

Tuna Couscous Salad

Preparation time: 10min / **Cooking time:** 0min / **Servings:** 6
Ingredients:
- 1 cup couscous
- 1 cup boiling water
- 420g can tuna in spring water, drained and flaked
- 420g can reduced-salt corn kernels, drained
- 2 cups frozen peas
- 4 spring onions (including green tops), finely sliced
- 1 cup fresh coriander, finely chopped
- 2 tablespoons sweet chilli sauce
- 1 tablespoon lemon juice
- 2 teaspoons curry powder, optional

Directions:
-Place couscous in a small heatproof bowl, pour over boiling water; cover and set aside for 3 minutes.
-In a large bowl combine the tuna, corn, peas, spring onions and coriander.
-Fluff couscous with a fork to separate grains and stir through sweet chilli sauce, lemon juice and curry powder.
-Add couscous mixture to salad ingredients, mix well and serve.

Nutrition: per 100g calories 489kcal ;protein 9g ;carbs 16g ; fiber 3g;

Chicken Stuffed Peppers

Preparation time: 10min / **Cooking time:** 35min / **Servings:** 4

Ingredients:
- 1 lb. boneless skinless chicken thighs or breasts, in 1/4-inch cubes
- 1 pint grape tomatoes, halved
- 2 cups cooked rice
- 2 Tbsp. all-purpose flour
- 2 Tbsp. red wine vinegar
- 2 Tbsp. olive oil
- 2 tsp. lemon juice
- 2 tsp. dried oregano
- 1 tsp. salt
- 1/2 tsp. garlic powder
- 1/4 tsp. black pepper
- 1/8 tsp. sugar
- 4 bell peppers
- 1 cup crumbled feta cheese, divided

Directions:
-Preheat oven to 400°F.
-In a large bowl mix the chicken, tomatoes, cooked rice, and flour.
-In a medium bowl whisk together red wine vinegar, olive oil, lemon juice, oregano, salt, garlic powder, black pepper, and sugar.
-Add vinegar mixture and 1/2 cup of the feta to the chicken and stir.
-Cut bell peppers in half from the stem end to the base and remove seeds and pith.
-Arrange peppers in baking dish. Fill with chicken mixture.
-Bake until chicken is cooked through to at least 165°F (use an instant-read thermometer to check), 35-40 minutes.

Nutrition:calories 831kcal ;protein 33g ;carbs 90g ; fat 37g ;

Zucchini Fritters with Feta, Cheddar, Mint and Parsley

Preparation time:30min / **Cooking time:** 45min / **Servings:** 10
Ingredients:
- 5 medium zucchinis, grated
- 1 cup onion, grated
- 1/2 tbsp salt
- 4-6 eggs
- 1 cup cheddar cheese, grated
- 1/2 cup feta cheese, grated
- 3-4 cups bread crumbs
- 1/2 cup fresh mint leaves, chopped
- 1 cup fresh parsley, chopped
- 1/4 tsp freshly ground pepper
- 1 cup Olive oil for frying

Directions:
-Place grated zucchini and onion in a colander. Add ½ Tablespoon salt, mix and let drain for 15-20 minutes. Squeeze out extra liquid with hands.
-In a large bowl, add 2 beaten eggs, cheddar and feta, 1 cup bread crumbs, mint, parsley, and ground pepper. Add zucchini/onion mixture. Mix ingredients with a fork. Continue adding breadcrumbs until fritters can be formed with your hands.
-Beat 2 eggs in a small bowl.
-In another bowl, add 1 cup breadcrumbs.
-Heat 1 cup of olive oil in a frying pan. Be careful not to overheat oil.
-Form fritters with mixture, dip in or brush with egg and then bread crumbs.
-Fry in olive oil. Drain on paper towels.

Nutrition:calories 436kcal ;protein 12g ;carbs 29g ; fat 31g ;

Stuffed Eggplants

Preparation time: 30min / **Cooking time:** 1.2h / **Servings:** 4

Ingredients:

- 2 large (about 350g each) eggplants
- 1 tbsp olive oil
- 1 onion, chopped
- 2 garlic cloves, crushed
- 2 tsp Moroccan seasoning
- 300g Coles lamb mince
- 1/2 cup basmati rice
- 3/4 cup Coles Brand Italian tomato passata
- 1/2 cup beef stock
- 100g feta, crumbled
- Spray olive oil
- 2 tbsp coriander leaves

Directions:

- Preheat oven to 200°C or 180°C fan. Halve eggplants lengthways. Cut a 1cm-wide border around the edge of each eggplant half. Score within the border in a diamond pattern. Use a melon baller or teaspoon to scoop out the flesh. Chop.
- Heat oil in a large deep frying pan over medium-high heat. Cook onion for 5 mins or until soft. Add the garlic and Moroccan seasoning. Cook, stirring, for 30 secs. Add the chopped eggplant. Cook for 5 mins or until soft. Add mince. Cook, stirring with a wooden spoon to break up any lumps, for 5 mins or until mince changes colour. Stir in rice, passata and stock. Season.
- Place the eggplant shells on a lightly greased oven tray, and fill with the mince mixture. Cover with foil and bake for 45 mins. Uncover, sprinkle with feta and spray with olive oil. Cook for a further 15 mins or until the eggplant is tender and the top is golden. Top with coriander.

Nutrition:calories 418kcal ;protein 24g ;carbs 34g;fat 21g;fiber7 g;

Salmon Bowl

Preparation time: 15min / **Cooking time:** 15min / **Servings:** 4

Ingredients:
- 1 cup dry rice of any type (or couscous for a quicker meal)
- 1 recipe Tahini Dressing or Miso Dressing
- 1 pound wild caught salmon fillets, skin on*
- Olive oil
- Kosher salt and fresh ground pepper
- 1 1/2 pounds fresh broccoli, stem on (about 3 large heads or 6 heaping cups florets)
- 1 teaspoon garlic powder
- ½ teaspoon onion powder
- ¼ teaspoon dry mustard powder (optional)

Directions:

-Make the rice: Start the rice (go to How to Make Rice or Instant Pot Rice).

-Mix the sauce: Make the Tahini Sauce or Miso Sauce (or make in advance and refrigerate).

-Broil the salmon: Preheat the broiler to high. Place a large sheet of aluminum foil on a baking sheet and brush it with olive oil. Pat each piece of salmon dry and place it on the foil skin side down. Brush salmon with a bit of olive oil and sprinkle with ½ teaspoon kosher salt (evenly divided among the fillets) and fresh ground pepper. Broil 4 to 5 minutes for very thin salmon or 7 to 10 minutes for 1-inch thick salmon, until it's just tender and pink at the center (the internal temperature should be between 125 to 130 degrees Fahrenheit in the center).

-Meanwhile, make the broccoli: Chop the broccoli into medium sized florets. In small bowl, mix together ¼ cup water with the garlic powder, onion powder and mustard powder. Add 3 tablespoons olive oil to a large skillet and heat it on medium high heat. Add broccoli and ½ teaspoon kosher salt. Cook 2 to 3 minutes until starting to brown, stirring occasionally. Reduce heat to medium, and add the water and spices. Cook an additional 4 to 5 minutes until fork tender, stirring occasionally. Taste and add additional salt and black pepper as necessary. Serve immediately.

Nutrition: calories 362kcal ;protein 30g ;carbs 32g ; fat 13g ;

Spicy Potato Salad

Preparation time: 15min / **Cooking time:** 20min / **Servings:** 9
Ingredients:
- 6 large red potatoes (about 3 pounds), cubed
- 1/3 cup vegetable oil
- 1/4 cup cider vinegar
- 1 tablespoon sugar
- 2-1/2 teaspoons chili powder
- 1-1/2 teaspoons hot pepper sauce
- 1 teaspoon salt
- 1/4 teaspoon onion powder
- 1/4 teaspoon ground cumin
- 1 can (15-1/4 ounces) whole kernel corn, drained
- 1 can (2-1/4 ounces) sliced ripe olives, drained
- 1/2 cup minced fresh cilantro
- 2 tablespoons chopped seeded jalapeno peppers

Directions:
-Place potatoes in a large saucepan and cover with water; cover and bring to a boil. Reduce heat; cook for 20-30 minutes or until tender. Drain and place in a large bowl.
-In a jar with a tight-fitting lid, combine the oil, vinegar, sugar, chili powder, hot pepper sauce, salt, onion powder and cumin; shake well. Pour over potatoes and toss to coat. Cover and refrigerate for at least 1 hour.
-Just before serving, stir in the corn, olives, cilantro and peppers.
Nutrition:calories 157kcal ;protein 3g ;carbs 26g ; fat 3g ; fiber 5g;

Chicken Rice Soup

Preparation time: 15min / **Cooking time:** 30min / **Servings:** 6
Ingredients:
- 1 tablespoon oil
- 1 onion minced
- 3 large carrots peeled and diced
- 1 stalk celery diced
- 1 teaspoon garlic minced
- 1 teaspoon dried parsley
- ½ teaspoon dried thyme
- 1 teaspoon salt
- ⅛ teaspoon black pepper
- 5 cups low sodium chicken broth
- 2 chicken breasts
- 1 cup brown rice
- 1 cup evaporated milk

Directions:
-In a large soup pot, heat oil over medium-high heat. Add onion, carrots and celery and cook and stir for 3-4 minutes, until onion begins to turn golden.
-Add garlic, parsley and thyme and cook 1 minute.
-Add salt and pepper, broth, chicken. Add rice. Stir and bring to a boil over medium-high heat.
-Reduce heat to medium-low (a simmer), cover, and cook for 30 minutes, stirring every 10 minutes, or until vegetables and rice are tender.
-Remove chicken from pot and shred. Add back to the pot with evaporated milk.

Nutrition:calories 332kcal ;protein 25g ;carbs 35g ; fat 9g ;

Chicken & Carrot Soup

Preparation time: 10min / **Cooking time:** 15min / **Servings:** 4
Ingredients:
- 1 tbsp – oil
- 1 - onion, chopped finely
- 2 - carrots, sliced
- 3 - stalks celery, cut into small size
- Salt as per taste
- Pepper as per taste
- 5 - cups chicken stock
- 2 - boneless chicken breast halves
-

Directions:
-Heat oil. Fry onion till transparent.
-Add chicken stock and bring to a boil.
-Add carrots, celery, chicken breast, and salt.
-Let it cook till the vegetables and chicken are tender (approximately
-10 minutes).
-Remove from fire. Remove chicken breast, and let it cool.
-Cut into bite-sized pieces. Add back to stock.
-Add pepper and bring back to a boil.

Nutrition: calories 240kcal ; fat 9g ;

Roasted Red Pepper Soup

Preparation time: 10min / **Cooking time:** 50min / **Servings:** 4

Ingredients:

- 6 red bell or pointed peppers (1.6 lbs/750g (around 6 peppers)
- 1 yellow onion
- 5 sun dried tomatoes jarred
- 4 garlic cloves peeled and whole
- 1 squeeze lemon juice (around ½ tablespoon)
- 2.5 cups vegetable stock (600ml)
- salt and pepper to season
- 1 tablespoon olive oil
- 1-2 tablespoon homemade pesto
- creme fraiche for topping

Directions:

-Pre-heat the oven to 200°C (400°F).

-Roughly chop the red peppers and place in a large baking tray with peeled whole garlic cloves. Drizzle with olive oil and sprinkle with salt and pepper then roast in the oven until slightly charred (around 40 minutes).

-Finely chop a white (yellow) onion and saute in a large pot with a little olive oil until translucent and soft. Once soft, add the roasted peppers and garlic, sun dried tomatoes and vegetable stock.

-Simmer for 10 minutes then turn off the heat and blend until completely smooth using an immersion blender. Taste for seasoning, I only add pepper because there's enough saltiness from the stock and sun dried tomatoes and pre seasoned peppers.

-Add a small splash of freshly squeezed lemon juice, stir and serve with a drizzle of creme fraiche and homemade pesto. Grab a hunk of crusty bread and dive in.

Nutrition: calories 107kcal ;protein 2g ;carbs 15g ; fat 4g ; fiber 4g;

Lentil Soup

Preparation time: 10min / **Cooking time:** 1h / **Servings:** 6

Ingredients:
- 1 onion, chopped
- ¼ cup olive oil
- 2 carrots, diced
- 2 stalks celery, chopped
- 2 cloves garlic, minced
- 1 teaspoon dried oregano
- 1 bay leaf
- 1 teaspoon dried basil
- 1 (14.5 ounce) can crushed tomatoes
- 2 cups dry lentils
- 8 cups water
- ½ cup spinach, rinsed and thinly sliced
- 2 tablespoons vinegar
- salt to taste
- ground black pepper to taste

Directions:

- In a large soup pot, heat oil over medium heat. Add onions, carrots, and celery; cook and stir until onion is tender. Stir in garlic, bay leaf, oregano, and basil; cook for 2 minutes.
- Stir in lentils, and add water and tomatoes. Bring to a boil. Reduce heat, and simmer for at least 1 hour. When ready to serve stir in spinach, and cook until it wilts. Stir in vinegar, and season to taste with salt and pepper, and more vinegar if desired.

Nutrition: calories 349kcal ; protein 18g ; carbs 48g ; fat 10g ;

White Bean Soup

Preparation time: 10min / **Cooking time:** 25min / **Servings:** 6
Ingredients:
- 1 tablespoon olive oil
- 1 large onion chopped
- 2 garlic cloves minced
- 2-3 large carrots chopped
- 2-3 celery rib chopped
- 6 cups vegetable broth
- 1 teaspoon dried thyme
- ½ teaspoon oregano
- 1 teaspoon salt
- ½ teaspoon black pepper
- 3 15-ounces canned white beans drained and rinsed
- 2 cups baby spinach
- Fresh parsley finely chopped, for serving
- Grated parmesan cheese for serving

Directions:
-In a large pot or saucepan, heat olive over medium high heat. Add onions and cook until onions are translucent, about 3-5 minutes. Add the garlic, carrots, celery, thyme, oregano, salt and pepper, and cook for an additional 2-3 minutes.

-Add vegetable broth and beans, bring to a boil, reduce heat and simmer for 15 minutes to combine all of the flavors together.

-Stir in the spinach and continue to simmer until the spinach wilts, about 2 minutes

-Remove from heat, sprinkle fresh parsley and grated parmesan cheese, if desired, and serve immediately.

Nutrition:calories 295kcal ;protein 17g ;carbs 52g ; fat 3g ;

Veggie Soup

Preparation time: 15min / **Cooking time:** 40min / **Servings:** 8
Ingredients:
- 2 Tbsp olive oil
- 1 1/2 cups chopped yellow onion (1 medium)
- 2 cups peeled and chopped carrots (about 5)
- 1 1/4 cups chopped celery (about 3)
- 4 cloves garlic , minced
- 4 (14.5 oz) cans low-sodium chicken broth or vegetable broth
- 2 (14.5 oz) cans diced tomatoes (undrained)
- 3 cups peeled and 1/2-inch thick diced potatoes (from about 3 medium)
- 1/3 cup chopped fresh parsley
- 2 bay leaves
- 1/2 tsp dried thyme, or 1 Tbsp fresh thyme leaves
- Salt and freshly ground black pepper
- 1 1/2 cups chopped frozen or fresh green beans
- 1 1/4 cups frozen or fresh corn
- 1 cup frozen or fresh peas

Directions:
-Heat olive oil in a large pot over medium-high heat.
-Add onions, carrots, and celery and saute 4 minutes then add garlic and saute 30 seconds longer.
-Add in broth, tomatoes, potatoes, parsley, bay leaves, thyme and season with salt and pepper to taste.*
-Bring to a boil, then add green beans.
-Reduce heat to medium-low, cover and simmer until potatoes are almost fully tender, about 20 - 30 minutes.
-Add corn and peas and cook 5 minutes longer. Serve warm.
Nutrition:calories 198kcal ;protein 7g ;carbs 31g ; fat 5g ; fiber 6g;

Seafood Gumbo

Preparation time: 20min / **Cooking time:** 30min / **Servings:**24
Ingredients:
- 1 cup all-purpose flour
- 1 cup canola oil
- 4 cups chopped onion
- 2 cups chopped celery
- 2 cups chopped green pepper
- 1 cup sliced green onions
- 4 cups chicken broth
- 8 cups water
- 4 cups sliced okra
- 2 tablespoons paprika
- 1 tablespoon salt
- 2 teaspoons oregano
- 1 teaspoon ground black pepper
- 6 cups small shrimp, rinsed and drained, or seafood of your choice
- 1 cup minced fresh parsley
- 2 tablespoons Cajun seasoning

Directions:
-In a heavy Dutch oven, combine flour and oil until smooth. Cook over medium-high heat for 5 minutes, stirring constantly. Reduce heat to medium. Cook and stir about 10 minutes more or until mixture is reddish brown.

-Add the onion, celery, green pepper and green onions; cook and stir for 5 minutes. Add the chicken broth, water, okra, paprika, salt, oregano and pepper. Bring to boil; reduce heat and simmer, covered, for 10 minutes.

-Add shrimp and parsley. Simmer, uncovered, about 5 minutes more or until seafood is done. Remove from heat; stir in Cajun seasoning.

Nutrition:calories 166kcal ;protein 10g ;carbs 10g ; fat 10g ; fiber 2g ;

Chicken Orzo Soup

Preparation time: 30min / **Cooking time:** 30min / **Servings:** 4
Ingredients:
-    1 carton (32 oz) Progresso™ chicken broth (4 cups)
-    1 lb boneless skinless chicken breasts
-    1 tablespoon olive oil
-    1 medium onion, chopped (1/2 cup)
-    ½ cup sliced carrots
-    ½ cup chopped celery
-    ¾ cup uncooked orzo or rosamarina pasta (4 1/2 oz)
-    2 cups water
-    ¼ cup chopped fresh parsley
-    Salt and pepper to taste

Directions:

-In 3-quart saucepan, heat broth and chicken to boiling; reduce heat. Simmer uncovered about 10 minutes until juice of chicken is clear when center of thickest part is cut (at least 165°F). Remove chicken to cutting board. Skim fat from broth, if necessary.
-Meanwhile, in 10-inch skillet, heat oil over medium heat. Cook onion, carrots and celery in oil, stirring occasionally, until tender.
-Add cooked vegetables, pasta and water to saucepan with broth. Heat to boiling; reduce heat. Simmer uncovered 8 to 10 minutes or until pasta is tender.
-Cut chicken into bite-size pieces. Add chicken and parsley to soup; heat until hot. Season with salt and pepper.

Nutrition:calories 330kcal ;protein 32g ;carbs 33g ; fat 8g ;

Zucchini Soup

Preparation time: 15min / **Cooking time:** 30min / **Servings:** 4
Ingredients:
- 2 tablespoon olive oil
- 1 small onion, finely chopped
- 2 garlic cloves, minced
- 4 medium zucchini (1 ½ to 2 pounds), skin on, ends trimmed, halved lengthwise, and sliced
- 3 cups vegetable or chicken broth, or more as desired for a thinner texture
- ¼ cup raw cashews
- 1 teaspoon kosher salt
- ¼ teaspoon ground black pepper
- 2 tablespoons fresh lemon juice
- 2 tablespoons chopped fresh herbs (dill, basil, or parsley work great), plus more for garnish

Directions:
-Heat the oil in a large pot over medium-high heat. Add the onion and saute for 4-5 minutes, until softened. Add the garlic, and stir for another minute.

-Add the zucchini, broth, cashews, salt, and pepper, and bring to a boil. Turn the heat down to low, cover, and simmer for about 15 to 20 minutes, or until the zucchini is tender.

- Add the chopped herbs and lemon juice to the soup. Then use an immersion blender (stick blender) to blend the soup until smooth, or transfer the soup in batches to a high-powered blender, and blend for just 15-30 seconds, until smooth.

- Ladle portions of the zucchini soup into bowls and garnish with a drizzle of olive oil and fresh herbs.

Nutrition:calories 167kcal ;protein 5g ;carbs 13g ; fat g ; fiber g ;

Tuscan Soup

Preparation time: 20min / **Cooking time:** 30min / **Servings:** 4
Ingredients:
- 6 cups chicken broth
- 1 onion, chopped
- 3 (3.5 ounce) links spicy Italian sausage
- 3 large potatoes, cubed
- 1 bunch fresh spinach, washed and chopped
- ¼ cup evaporated milk
- salt to taste
- ground black pepper to taste

Directions:
-Remove skin from sausage and crumble into frying pan. Add chopped onion, and cook over medium heat until meat is no longer pink. If you are trying to cut fat, remove meat from pan, place in a colander, and rinse under cold water.
-Place meat in a large pot; add stock and potatoes. Boil until potato is cooked.
-Add spinach. Continue boiling until spinach is lightly cooked.
-Remove soup from heat, stir in evaporated milk, and season to taste. Do not add any salt if using canned stock.

Nutrition:calories 559kcal ;protein 26g ;carbs 57g ; fat 25g ;

Cauliflower Cream Sauce

Preparation time: 10min / **Cooking time:** 10min / **Servings:** 5
Ingredients:
- 1 head of cauliflower, roughly chopped
- 2 cups vegetable broth
- 2 cups non-dairy milk (such as soy or almond)
- 3 cloves garlic, peeled
- ¼ cup nutritional yeast
- 2 teaspoons white miso paste
- ½ teaspoon salt (or to taste)

Directions:
-Add the cauliflower, vegetable broth, non-dairy milk, and garlic to a big pot, and bring to a simmer. Cook for about 10 minutes, until the cauliflower is very soft and falls apart when pierced with a fork.
-Now blend up the cauliflower mixture. You can use an emersion blender and blend everything together directly in the pot, or you can use a standing blender and blend the cauliflower and cooking liquid in batches, being careful not to fill the blender too high so the hot liquid doesn't explode out the top. Add the nutritional yeast, white miso paste, and salt and blend to combine.
-If you find your sauce is too thin, return the sauce to the pan and cook it down a bit more stirring often so it doesn't burn. If it is too thick, add a bit more vegetable broth or water.
-The ways to use this sauce are endless. Toss with pasta, mix into a casserole, top on pizza, make creamy scalloped potatoes, drizzle over baked potatoes, use in lasagna, you name it!

Nutrition:calories 52kcal ;

White Bean Soup with Orange Slices and Olive Oil

Preparation time: 15min / **Cooking time:** 30min / **Servings:** 8

Ingredients:
- 4 large carrots, sliced thin
- 5 celery sticks, sliced thin
- 1 large onion, sliced thin
- 1 cup extra virgin olive oil
- 1/2 tsp dried oregano
- 1 bay leaf
- 3 slices orange (skin and flesh)
- 2 tbsp tomato paste
- 15 ounces cannellini (white) beans 4 cans
- 2 cups water

Directions:
-Sauté carrots, celery, and onion in olive oil on medium heat until soft.Add oregano and bay leaf.
-Add orange slices and tomato paste. Sauté for 2 minutes
-Add Cannellini beans, 2 cans with liquid, 2 cans drained. Add 2 cups water.
-Simmer for 30-40 minutes until soup thickens, stirring occasionally.

Nutrition:calories 324kcal ;protein 5g ;carbs 17g ; fat 27g ; fiber 4g ;

Zucchini-Basil Soup

Preparation time: 15min / **Cooking time:** 30min / **Servings:** 5
Ingredients:
- 2 pounds zucchini, trimmed and cut crosswise into thirds
- 3/4 cup chopped onion
- 2 garlic cloves, chopped
- 1/4 cup olive oil
- 4 cups water, divided
- 1/3 cup packed basil leaves

Directions:
-Julienne skin (only) from half of zucchini with slicer; toss with 1/2 teaspoon salt and drain in a sieve until wilted, at least 20 minutes. Coarsely chop remaining zucchini.
-Cook onion and garlic in oil in a 3- to 4-quarts heavy saucepan over medium-low heat, stirring occasionally, until softened, about 5 minutes. Add chopped zucchini and 1 teaspoon salt and cook, stirring occasionally, 5 minutes. Add 3 cups water and simmer, partially covered, until tender, about 15 minutes. Purée soup with basil in 2 batches in a blender (use caution when blending hot liquids).
-Bring remaining cup water to a boil in a small saucepan and blanch julienned zucchini 1 minute. Drain in a sieve set over a bowl (use liquid to thin soup if necessary).
-Season soup with salt and pepper. Serve in shallow bowls with julienned zucchini mounded on top.
Nutrition: calories 200kcal ; carbs 18g ;

Chicken and Leek Soup

Preparation time: 15min / **Cooking time:** 45min / **Servings:** 7
Ingredients:
- 2 1/2 lbs frying chickens, cut up
- 4 cups water
- 1 medium carrot, sliced
- 1 stalk celery, sliced
- 1/2 cup barley
- 2 teaspoons chicken bouillon
- 2 teaspoons salt
- 1/4 teaspoon pepper
- 1 bay leaf
- 1 1/2 cups leeks, with tops (sliced and cleaned very well)

Directions:
-Heat all ingredients except leeks to boiling in large stockpot or Dutch oven.
-Reduce heat, cover and simmer 30 minutes.
-Add leeks.
-Bring back to a boil; reduce heat.
-Cover and simmer until thickest pieces of chicken are done, about 15 minutes.
-Remove chicken from broth and cool slightly; remove chicken from bones and skin.
-Skim fat from both and remove bay leaf.
-Cut chicken into 1 inch pieces and return to broth.
-Heat about 5 minutes; serve.

Nutrition:calories 412kcal ;protein 32g ;carbs 13g ; fat 24g ; fiber 3g ;

Lemon Lamb Soup

Preparation time: 15min / **Cooking time:** 40min / **Servings:**11
Ingredients:
- 5 large shoulder lamb chops, with bone in
- 12 cups water
- 1 fennel bulb, chopped 1/2 inch pieces
- 5 potatoes, chopped 1/2 inc cubes
- 1 whole lemon
- 1/2 - 3/4 cup fresh curly-leaf parsley, chopped
- 1 -2 tablespoon salt, to taste

Directions:
-Add water and salt and bring to boil.
-Add Lamb to boiling water. 30 minutes(you can debone the meat and cut to cubes first but add bones in water with the meat cubes I prefer to cube the meat after its boiled).
-Remove the meat and/or bones and the goop on top of boiling water.
-add the chopped fennel and boil for 5 minutes Med/high heat.
-add the potatoes and boil for 10 minutes.
-Re introduce the meat if you have not cubed it first and boil 5 minutes.
-Add the parsley and boil for 5 minutes.
-Squeeze the juice of the lemon into the soup watching for the seeds and boil for another 10 minutes.

Nutrition:calories 92kcal ;protein 3g ;carbs 21g ; fat 4g ; fiber 1g ;

Banana Smoothie Bowl

Preparation time: 10min / **Cooking time:** 0min / **Servings:** 1
Ingredients:
- 2 frozen bananas, peeled and sliced
- ¼ cup milk – almond, soy, etc.
- 1–2 tablespoons nut butter
- Pinch cinnamon, optional
-

Directions:
-Add the bananas to the blender. Let it sit in the blender for 2-3 minutes to soften slightly. Turn the blender on low and let it slowly chop up the fruit into small pieces.
-Add in the milk and blend, starting on low and working the speed up slowly, until smooth. Use a tamper or scrape down the sides as needed.
-Spoon the smoothie into a bowl and add on your desired toppings.

Nutrition:calories 325kcal ;protein 7g ;carbs 57g ; fat 10g ; fiber 7g ;

Lemon Bars

Preparation time: 20min / **Cooking time:** 40min / **Servings:**15
Ingredients:
- 2 c. flour
- 1/2 c. sugar
- 1/4 tsp. salt
- 2 sticks (1 cup) salted butter, cut into small cubes

For the filling:
- 1 1/2 c. sugar
- 1/4 c. flour
- 4 whole large eggs
- Zest and juice of 4 medium-sized lemons
- Powdered sugar, for sifting

Directions:
-For the crust: Preheat the oven to 350°. Grease a 9-by-13-inch pan with butter. (Use an 8 x 10 pan if you'd like the layers to be a little thicker.)
-Stir together the flour, sugar, and salt. Add the butter to the bowl and use a pastry cutter to cut it all together until the mixture resembles fine crumbs. Press into the prepared pan and bake until golden around the edges, about 20 minutes.
-For the filling: Stir together the sugar and flour. Crack in the eggs and whisk to combine. Add the lemon zest and juice and mix until combined. Pour over the crust and bake about 20 minutes.
-Allow to cool in the fridge for a minimum of 2 hours, then sift powdered sugar over the top before cutting into squares.
Nutrition: 1 bar calories 290kcal ;

Blackberry and Apple Cobbler

Preparation time: 15min / **Cooking time:** 45min / **Servings:** 8
Ingredients:
- 1/4 cup butter (softened)
- 1/3 cup sugar
- 1 cup all-purpose flour (sifted)
- 2 teaspoons baking powder
- 1/4 teaspoon salt
- 1/2 cup milk
- 2 cups blackberries
- 1 cup apples (diced)
- 1/2 cup sugar (plus more for sprinkling)

Directions:
-Gather the ingredients.
-Heat the oven to 375 F / 190 C / Gas 5. Butter a 9-inch round cake pan.
-Cream the butter and 1/3 cup sugar until light and fluffy.
-Sift together the flour, baking powder, and salt.
-Add dry ingredients to creamed mixture alternating with the milk; beat until smooth.
-In a separate bowl, combine blackberries, apples, and 1/2 cup sugar. Let stand for 5 minutes.
-Put fruit mixture in the prepared cake pan. Pour batter over the fruit.
-Sprinkle with a little sugar.
-Bake in the preheated oven for 45 to 50 minutes.
-Serve warm with cream or ice cream.

Nutrition:calories 227kcal ;protein 3g ;carbs 36g ; fat 9g ;

Green tea and vanilla ice cream

Preparation time: 10min / **Cooking time:** 3h / **Servings:** 8

Ingredients:
- 1/2 (14.1-oz.) package refrigerated piecrusts (1 piecrust)
- 3 cups fresh figs, stemmed and quartered (about 15 oz.)
- 4 large eggs, beaten
- 3/4 cup granulated sugar
- 1/4 cup all-purpose flou
- 1/4 cup unsalted butter, melted
- 2 tablespoons fresh lemon juice (from 1 lemon)
- 2 teaspoons ground ginger
- Whipped cream

Directions:
-Preheat oven to 425°F. Fit piecrust into a 9-inch pie plate, pressing into bottom and up sides. Fold edges under, and crimp, if desired. Spread figs in an even layer in piecrust. Combine eggs, sugar, flour, butter, lemon juice, and ginger in a medium bowl, and stir vigorously until well blended. Pour over figs in piecrust.
-Bake on bottom rack of preheated oven for 10 minutes. Reduce temperature to 350°F; bake until center is set, about 40 minutes more. Cool completely on a wire rack, about 2 hours. Serve with whipped cream.

Nutrition: calories 350kcal ;

Cherry Cream

Preparation time: 15min / **Cooking time:** 0min / **Servings:** 10
Ingredients:
- 1 package (8 ounces) cream cheese, softened
- 1 can (20 ounces) crushed pineapple, undrained
- 1 can (21 ounces) cherry pie filling
- 1/2 cup chopped pecans
- 1 carton (8 ounces) frozen whipped topping, thawed
- Additional whipped topping and cherries, optional

Directions:
-In a large bowl, beat cream cheese and pineapple. Stir in pie filling and pecans. Fold in whipped topping. Spoon into individual dessert dishes. Garnish each with additional whipped topping and a cherry if desired. Cover and chill until serving.

Nutrition:calories 296kcal ;protein 3g ;carbs 36g ; fat 16g ; fiber 1g ;

Strawberries and Cream

Preparation time: 10min / **Cooking time:** 0min / **Servings:** 8
Ingredients:
- 32 ounces fresh strawberries , hulled
- 16 ounces sour cream (or plain greek yogurt)
- 2/3 cup evaporated milk
- 2/3 cup heavy whipping cream
- 14 ounces sweetened condensed milk , la lechera
- 1 tablespoon vanilla extract

Directions:
-Slice the strawberries into thin slices.
-Add the sour cream, evaporated milk, heavy cream, sweetened condensed milk and vanilla to a mixing bowl. Beat with electric mixers for 2 minutes.
-Spoon ½ cup of fresh sliced strawberries into a cup. Pour ½ cup of the cream mixture over the top.
-Serve with whipped cream on top, if desired.
-Serves 8 (1 cup servings)

Nutrition:calories 331kcal ;protein 12g ;carbs 41g ; fat 14g ; fiber 2g ;

Plum or Apple Cake

Preparation time: 20min / **Cooking time:** 30min / **Servings:**15
Ingredients:
- 400g of chopped fruit of choice (can be fresh, frozen, or tinned)*
- 2 cups of self raising flour
- ½ cup of sugar
- 1 teaspoon of ground cinnamon
- 125g of melted butter
- ⅓ cup of milk
- 1 egg
- 1 teaspoon of vanilla extract
- 1 – 2 tablespoons of extra sugar for sprinkling on top (optional)

Directions:
-Line a 20cm x 30cm (8 x 12 inch) rectangular slice tin with baking paper and preheat oven to 180 °C (350 °F).
-Place the flour, sugar, and cinnamon into a large mixing bowl and stir to combine.
-Add the fruit and stir to coat.
-Now add in the butter, milk, egg, and vanilla and mix thoroughly.
-Press mixture into prepared tin and sprinkle with extra sugar if using.
-Bake for 30 – 35 minutes or until golden brown and a cake tester/toothpick inserted into the middle comes out clean.
-Allow to cool in tin completely before removing and slicing.
Nutrition:calories 174kcal ;protein 2g ;carbs 25g ; fat 8g ; fiber 1g ;

Cinnamon Chickpea Blondies

Preparation time: 10min / **Cooking time:** 30min / **Servings:** 9
Ingredients:
- 1 can (15 ounces) chickpeas drained and rinsed (or 1.5 cups cooked chickpeas)
- ½ cup cashew butter
- ¼ cup old fashioned rolled oats certified gluten free if desired
- ⅔ cup coconut sugar or organic brown sugar
- ¼ cup pure maple syrup
- 1 ½ tablespoons ground cinnamon
- 1 teaspoon pure vanilla extract
- ½ teaspoon baking powder
- ¼ teaspoon baking soda
- ¼ teaspoon salt
- ¼ cup chopped walnuts optional
- Cinnamon Sugar mixture optional for garnish (equal parts of cinnamon and sugar mixed together)

Directions:
-Preheat oven to 350°F.
-Lightly spritz an 8×8 baking dish with oil or line with parchment paper.
-Combine all ingredients, except walnuts, in the bowl of a food processor and puree until smooth.
-Pour the batter into the prepared baking dish.
-Add the walnuts, if using, and stir gently, then smooth the batter out.
-Sprinkle with cinnamon sugar mixture, if using.
-Bake for 30 minutes until the sides start to pull away from the baking dish and the top is firm.
-The blondies will continue to firm up while cooling.
-Cut into equal size squares and serve.

Nutrition: calories 246kcal ;protein 35g ;carbs 6g ; fat 8g ; fiber 4g ;

Cocoa Brownies

Preparation time: 30min / **Cooking time:** 30min / **Servings:** 1
Ingredients:
- 170 grams (3/4 cup) butter, melted
- 200 grams (1 cup) caster sugar or granulated sugar
- 90 grams (1/2 cup) brown sugar
- 2 teaspoons vanilla extract
- 4 large eggs
- 40 grams (1/2 cup) cocoa powder, sifted
- 70 grams (1/2 cup) plain flour or all purpose flour
- Pinch of salt
- 75 grams (1/2 cup) chocolate chips, optional

Directions:
-Preheat oven to 180 C (350 F) standard / 160 C (320 F) fan-forced. Grease and line an 8 inch square baking tin with baking or parchment paper, ensuring two sides overhang.
-In a large mixing bowl, add the melted butter, sugars and vanilla and whisk together. Add the eggs, one at a time, whisking well after each one.
-Add cocoa powder, flour and salt. Whisk well until you have a thick and creamy chocolate brownie batter. Stir through chocolate chips, if using.
-Pour the brownie batter into the prepared tin and place in the oven. Bake brownies for approximately 25-30 minutes or until they no longer wobble in the middle. Transfer to a wire rack to cool completely.

Nutrition:calories 220kcal ;

Almond and Cardamom Cream Pudding

Preparation time: 5min / **Cooking time:** 20min / **Servings:** 6
Ingredients:
- 3 cups milk
- 1 pinch salt
- ⅓ cup sugar granulated
- ½ cup cornstarch
- ¼ cup water cold
- ½ cup almonds
- slivered, blanched
- ¼ teaspoon cardamom seeds ground
- ¼ teaspoon saffron threads pounded
- ¼ cup pistachio nuts

Directions:
-Put all but ½ cup milk into a heavy pan and add salt and sugar.
-Put on to heat gently, stirring to dissove sugar.
-Blend cornflour into reserved milk with the ¼ cup water and pour into warm milk, stirring constantly.
-Add almonds and keep stirring until mixture thickens and bubbles.
-Use a whisk if mixture becomes lumpy.
-Add cardamom to taste and the pounded saffron.
-Cook on low heat for 5 minutes, letting pudding simmer very gently.
-Stir occasionally.
-Pour into 6 or 8 individual sweet dishes, spreading evenly.
-Sprinkle pistachio nuts around edge of each dish.
-To serve firnee in the traditional manner, the pudding should be poured into two plates, decorated with pistachio nuts and cut into quarters to serve in wedges.

Nutrition:calories 167kcal ;protein 12g ;carbs 9g ; fat 5g ; fiber 1g ;

Banana Cupcakes with Honey-Cinnamon Frosting

Preparation time: 10min / **Cooking time:** 30min / **Servings:**12
Ingredients:
- 1 1/2 cups all-purpose flour, (spooned and leveled)
- 3/4 cup sugar
- 1 teaspoon baking powder
- 1/2 teaspoon baking soda
- 1/4 teaspoon salt
- 1/2 cup (1 stick) unsalted butter, melted
- 1 1/2 cups mashed bananas (about 4 ripe bananas), plus 1 whole banana, for garnish (optional)
- 2 large eggs
- 1/2 teaspoon pure vanilla extract
- Honey-Cinnamon Frosting

Directions:
-Preheat oven to 350 degrees. Line a standard 12-cup muffin pan with paper liners. In a medium bowl, whisk together flour, sugar, baking powder, baking soda, and salt.
-Make a well in center of flour mixture. In well, mix together butter, mashed bananas, eggs, and vanilla. Stir to incorporate flour mixture (do not overmix). Dividing evenly, spoon batter into muffin cups.
-Bake until a toothpick inserted in center of a cupcake comes out clean, 25 to 30 minutes. Remove cupcakes from pan; cool completely on a wire rack. Spread tops with honey-cinnamon frosting. Just before serving, peel and slice banana into rounds, and place one on each cupcake, if desired.
Nutrition:calories 200kcal ;

Apple and Rhubarb Cream

Preparation time: 10min / **Cooking time:** 15min / **Servings:** 2

Ingredients:
- 300ml cream
- ¼ cup (40g) icing sugar mixture
- 1 tablespoon Cointreau, Grand Marnier or brandy
- 410g can pie apple and rhubarb
- 20g butter
- 1 tablespoon golden syrup
- ½ cup (15g) corn flakes

Directions:
-Beat the cream, sugar and liqueur in a small bowl with an electric mixer until soft peaks form.

-Gently fold in the apple and rhubarb. Spoon the mixture into four 1-cup (250ml) capacity glasses.

-Combine butter and golden syrup in small saucepan; stir over low heat until the butter is melted. Add corn flakes and cook, stirring, for about 2 minutes or until browned lightly.

-Divide corn flake mixture evenly over apple and rhubarb cream.

Nutrition:calories 420kcal ;

Almond Rice Pudding with Cherry Sauce

Preparation time: 10min / **Cooking time:** 40min / **Servings:** 6
Ingredients:
For the Rice Pudding:
- 1 cup arborio rice
- 1 1/4 cup water
- 4 cups milk
- 1/4 teaspoon salt
- 2 teaspoons finely grated lemon zest
- 2 tablespoons sugar
- 4 ounces chopped blanched almonds

For the Risalamande:
- 2 cups heavy whipping cream
- 1/4 cup sugar
- 2 teaspoons vanilla bean paste *not extract*
- 1/2 teaspoon quality almond extract
- Cherry Sauce warm, for serving (click the link for the cherry sauce recipe)
- Sprigs of fresh mint for garnish optional

Directions:

-Bring the rice, salt, lemon zest, sugar and water to a boil in a medium-sized stock pot. Boil for 3 minutes, add the milk and return to a boil. Reduce the heat to low, cover and simmer for 30-35 minutes, stirring occasionally, increasing the frequency during the last 10 minutes to prevent scorching. Stir in the chopped blanched almonds.

-Let the rice cool and then chill for several hours or overnight.

-Beat the cream until it starts to thicken. Add the sugar, vanilla bean paste and almond extract and beat until stiff peaks form. Be careful not to over-beat. Stir the cream mixture into the rice pudding.(Note: The rice will may be very stiff. Stir it to loosen it up and then stir it more after the cream has been added to break up any clumps.)

-Serve the Risalamande at room temperature with the warm cherry sauce.

Nutrition:calories 656kcal ;protein 12g ;carbs 53g ; fat 44g ; fiber 3g ;

Peach Sorbet

Preparation time: 5min / **Cooking time:** 10min / **Servings:** 4
Ingredients:
- 4 medium peaches, sliced (approx. 3 1/2 cups)
- 1 tbsp. raw honey
- 1 tsp. lemon juice
- 1/4 cup warm water, as needed

Directions:
-Slice the ripe peaches and remove the pit.
-Lay out the fresh peach slices over a rimmed baking sheet lined with parchment paper.
-Freeze the peach slices until completely solid, which should take at least 3-4 hours, or overnight.
-Place the frozen peach slices into the bowl of a food processor or heavy duty blender, along with a little raw honey, and freshly squeezed lemon juice.
-Blend until smooth.
-You may need to add a little warm water and press down with a spatula to help the process along.
-Eat immediately for a softer texture, or transfer into a freezer-safe container and freeze for 3-4 hours or until firm.

Nutrition:calories 70kcal ;protein 1g ;carbs 17g ; fiber 2g ;

Cranberry Pear Pie

Preparation time: 20min / **Cooking time:** 50min / **Servings:** 8
Ingredients:
- Pastry for single-crust pie (9 inches)
- 2 tablespoons all-purpose flour
- 1/2 cup maple syrup
- 2 tablespoons butter, melted
- 5 cups sliced peeled fresh pears
- 1 cup fresh or frozen cranberries

Topping:
- 1/2 cup all-purpose flour
- 1/4 cup packed brown sugar
- 1 teaspoon ground cinnamon
- 1/3 cup cold butter, cubed
- 1/2 cup chopped walnuts

Directions:
-Line a 9-in. pie plate with pastry; trim and flute edges. Set aside. In a large bowl, combine the flour, syrup and butter until smooth. Add pears and cranberries; toss to coat. Spoon into crust.

-For topping, combine the flour, brown sugar and cinnamon; cut in butter until crumbly. Stir in walnuts. Sprinkle over filling.

-Cover edges of crust loosely with foil to prevent overbrowning. Bake at 400° for 15 minutes. Reduce heat to 350°. Remove foil; bake 35-40 minutes longer or until crust is golden brown and filling is bubbly. Cool on a wire rack.

Nutrition:calories 483kcal ;protein 5g ;carbs 59g ; fat 27g ; fiber 5g ;

Lemon Cream

Preparation time: 20min / **Cooking time:** 10min / **Servings:** 2
Ingredients:
- 155g (2/3 cup) lemon juice
- zest of 2 lemons
- 165 g (3/4 cup) granulated sugar
- 100 g (2 large) eggs
- 40 g (2 large) egg yolks
- pinch of salt
- 226 g (8 oz) unsalted butter, diced and at room temperature

Directions:
-Place the lemon juice, zest, sugar, eggs, egg yolks, and salt into a medium heatproof bowl set over a small saucepan filled with an inch of simmering water. Whisk constantly until the mixture thickens, about 10 minutes. The temperature should read 170°F/75°C, and the mixture should coat the back of a wooden spoon.
-Pour through a fine sieve into a blender. Allow the cream to cool for about 15 minutes (the temperature should be approximately 140°F/60°C).
-Blend the butter into the lemon mixture, a couple of pieces at a time. Once all the butter has been added and incorporated, pour the lemon filling into a container. Place a sheet of plastic wrap directly onto the surface of the filling to prevent a 'skin' from forming. Refrigerate for at least 4 hours before enjoying.
Nutrition:calories 188kcal ;protein 1g ;carbs 27g ; fat 8g ;

Apple and Blueberry Stew

Preparation time: 5min / **Cooking time:** 0min / **Servings:** 5

Ingredients:
- 1 medium apple, peeled, cored and chopped
- 60g frozen blueberries
- 150ml water

Directions:
-Put the chopped apple and blueberries into a saucepan, add 150ml water.
-Cook for around 10 minutes until the apple and blueberry are completely soft. If it sticks to the pan, add a little more water.
-Pour the mixture into a bowl and stir.
-Cool down and then serve.

Nutrition:calories 190kcal ;

Mandarin Cream

Preparation time: 5min / **Cooking time:** 12min / **Servings:** 16
Ingredients:
Crust:
- 9 tablespoons butter or stick margarine, softened
- ½ cup sugar
- 1 teaspoon vanilla extrac
- 1 ½ cups all-purpose flour
- ⅛ teaspoon salt
- Cooking spray

Filling:
- 2 (11-ounce) cans mandarin oranges in light syrup, undrained
- ¼ cup sugar
- 1 (16-ounce) carton fat-free sour cream
- 1 (8-ounce) carton low-fat sour cream
- 2 (3.4-ounce) packages vanilla instant pudding mix or 2 (1.4-ounce) packages sugar-free vanilla instant pudding mix
- 1 (8-ounce) container frozen reduced-calorie whipped topping, thawed
- Mint sprigs (optional)

Directions:
-To prepare crust, combine the butter, 1/2 cup sugar, and vanilla in a large bowl. Beat at medium speed of a mixer until light and fluffy (about 2 minutes). Lightly spoon flour into dry measuring cups; level with a knife. Add flour and salt to butter mixture, beating at low speed until well-blended.
-Preheat oven to 400°.
-Pat dough into a 13 x 9-inch baking dish coated with cooking spray, and pierce bottom of dough with a fork. Bake at 400° for 12 minutes or until lightly browned. Cool crust on a wire rack.
-To prepare filling, drain mandarin oranges over a large bowl, reserving 1/2 cup juice. Combine juice, 1/4 cup sugar, sour creams, and pudding mix in a large bowl. Stir in the orange segments. Spoon orange mixture over crust, spreading evenly. Top with whipped topping. Chill 1 hour. Garnish with mint, if desired.

Nutrition: calories 276kcal ;carbs 43g ; fat 9g ;

Strawberries with Mint Whipped Cream

Preparation time: 10min / **Cooking time:** 10min / **Servings:** 4

Ingredients:
- 1/4 cup sugar
- 2 packed cups fresh mint leaves and stems, coarsely chopped, plus sprigs for garnish
- 1 cup heavy cream
- 1 quart strawberries, hulled and thinly sliced
-

Directions:
-Make syrup: In a medium saucepan over medium heat, bring sugar, mint, and 2 tablespoons water to a boil. Remove from heat; steep 15 minutes. Strain through a fine-mesh sieve into a measuring cup, pressing to extract as much liquid as possible. Discard solids. Let cool (makes about 1/4 cup).
-Meanwhile, in a large bowl, whip cream until stiff peaks form. Gently fold in 1/4 cup syrup (store any remaining syrup); if needed, re-whip cream to stiffen.
-Starting with strawberries, spoon alternating layers of strawberries and cream into four serving glasses. Top each with a mint sprig.

Nutrition:calories 230kcal ;

Vanilla Cake

Preparation time: 15min / **Cooking time:** 30min / **Servings:**14
Ingredients:
- 2 1/2 cups all-purpose flour
- 1 Tbsp baking powder
- 1/2 tsp fine salt
- 1 cup unsalted butter, softened
- 1 1/2 cups granulated sugar
- 4 large eggs, room temperature
- 4 tsp pure vanilla extract
- 1 cup buttermilk, or plain kefir, room temperature

Directions:
-Preheat oven to 350°F. Butter and flour two 9" cake pans, tapping out excess flour.

-In a medium bowl, whisk together flour, baking powder and salt. Set flour mixture aside.

-In a large mixing bowl using an electric hand mixer (or stand mixer), beat butter and sugar on medium-high speed for 5 minutes until thick and fluffy, scraping down the bowl as needed.

-Add 4 eggs, one at a time, beating well with each addition then scrape down the bowl. Add 4 tsp vanilla extract and beat to combine.

-Reduce mixer to medium speed and add the flour mixture in thirds alternating with the 1 cup of room temperature buttermilk, allowing the flour and buttermilk to incorporate with each addition. Scrape down the bowl as needed and beat until just combined and smooth.

-Divide batter evenly between 2 prepared cake pans and spread out the batter into the pans smoothing out the tops with a spatula. Bake on the center rack at 350°F for 28-30 minutes. Rest in pans for 10 minutes then run a knife or thin spatula around the edges to loosen and turn out onto a wire rack to cool completely before applying Vanilla Frosting.

Nutrition:calories 313kcal ;protein 5g ;carbs 40g ; fat 1g ; fiber 15g ;

Pumpkin Cream Sandwiches

Preparation time: 20min / **Cooking time:** 10min / **Servings:** 8
Ingredients:
- 3 tablespoons unsalted butter, at room temperature
- ⅓ cup brown sugar
- ¼ cup granulated sugar
- ½ cup canned pumpkin puree
- ½ teaspoon pure vanilla extract
- 1 large egg
- 1 cup all-purpose flour
- ½ teaspoon baking powder
- ¼ teaspoon baking soda
- ½ teaspoon pumpkin pie spice (found in the spice aisle)
- ¼ teaspoon kosher salt
- ⅔ cup cream cheese, at room temperature
- ¼ cup heavy cream
- ¼ cup confectioners' sugar

Directions:
-Heat oven to 375° F.
-Beat the butter, brown sugar, and granulated sugar in the bowl of an electric mixer fitted with a paddle attachment until smooth. Add the pumpkin, vanilla, and egg and beat until combined.
-Combine the flour, baking powder, baking soda, pumpkin pie spice, and salt in a medium bowl. Slowly add the flour mixture to the sugar and butter and beat on medium-low speed until fully incorporated.
-Spoon heaping tablespoons of the mixture 2 inches apart onto parchment- or foil-lined baking sheets. Bake until puffed and cooked through, about 10 minutes. Let cool for 5 minutes.
-Clean the mixer, then, as the cookies bake, beat the cream cheese, heavy cream, and confectioners' sugar until smooth. Spread the flat sides of half the cooled cookies with the cream mixture. Top with the remaining cookies.

Nutrition: calories 258kcal ;protein 4g ;carbs 29g ; fat 15g ; fiber 1g ;

Berry Smoothie Bowl

Preparation time: 19min / **Cooking time:** 0min / **Servings:** 2
Ingredients:
- ½ cup strawberry (75 g)
- ½ cup raspberry (60 g)
- 1 cup blackberry (55 g)
- 1 banana, sliced
- ½ cup greek yogurt (140 g)
- ¼ cup almond milk (60 mL), or soy milk
- ¼ cup peanut butter (60 g)

Directions:
-Add the berries, banana, Greek yogurt, almond milk, and peanut butter to a blender and blend until smooth.
-Top with your favorite toppings.
-Nutrition Calories: 1709 Fat: 130 grams Carbs: 108 grams Fiber: 37 grams Sugars: 48 grams Protein: 57 grams

Nutrition:calories 471kcal ;protein 17g ;carbs 60g ; fat 21g ; fiber 14g ;

Coconut Mint Ice Cream

Preparation time: 5min / **Cooking time:** 3h / **Servings:** 4
Ingredients:
2 cans full fat coconut milk, chilled
1/3 cup raw honey
1 whole avocado
1 teaspoon peppermint extract
3/4 cup chocolate chips
Directions:
-Place the freezer bowl of your ice cream maker into the freezer the day
before you plan to make ice cream.
-Scoop the chilled coconut cream from the cans, leave out the liquid.
-Remove the pit and peel from the avocado.
-In a food process place the coconut cream, avocado, raw honey and
peppermint extract in a bowl of a food processor, blend until smooth.
-Transfer coconut milk mixture to an ice cream maker bowl, follow the
instructions on your ice cream maker and churn until the ice cream is thick
and smooth.
-With the mixer still running, add in the chocolate chips and process until
just combined.
-Once the ice cream is firm, remove from the ice cream maker and place in
a freezer-safe bowl or container. Freeze for at least 3 hours to allow the ice
cream to harden.
-Before serving, allow ice cream to sit out at room temperature for 5-10
minutes until it's soft enough to scoop.
Nutrition:calories 595kcal ;protein 5g ;carbs 37g ; fat 50g ; fiber 4g ;

Watermelon Ice-Cream

Preparation time: 10min / **Cooking time:** 4h / **Servings:** 4
Ingredients:
- 3 cups cubed watermelon
- 1 cup vanilla almond milk*
- 2 tablespoons monk fruit*

Directions:
-Line a quarter sheet pan with parchement paper.
-Cut watermelon into uniform, cubes and place on lined sheet pan. Place in the freezer for four hours (or until frozen through).
-Remove watermelon from freezer and pop into a high speed blender with the almond milk and monk fruit.
-Blend until the watermelon has broken down and you have a thick, creamy consistency. If you were going to eat it right away (which is my favorite way to enjoy this), serve and enjoy!
-If you want to eat the watermelon ice-cream later, transfer to a loaf pan and place back in the freezer. Note: if you want to fill the loaf pan, you need to make two batches of ice-cream.
-When you are ready to eat your ice-cream, let it sit at room temperature for ten minutes before scooping. Once it softens a bit, serve and enjoy.

Nutrition:calories 43kcal ;protein 1g ;carbs 9g ; fat 1g ; fiber 1g ;

Chocolate Cherry Cream

Preparation time: 10min / **Cooking time:** 0min / **Servings:** 24

Ingredients:
- 1 cup semi-sweet chocolate chips
- 1/3 cup evaporated milk
- 1 1/2 cups sifted powdered sugar
- 1/3 cup chopped nuts
- 1/3 cup chopped maraschino cherry, , well drained
- 1 1/4 cups coconut or 1 1/4 cups chopped nuts

Directions:
-Melt chocolate and milk over low heat.
-Remove from heat.
-Stir in powdered sugar, nuts and cherries, mix well.
-Chill until cool enough to handle.
-Shape into 1-inch balls and roll in nuts or coconut.
-Chill at least 4 hours.

Nutrition:calories 108kcal ;protein 1g ;carbs 13g ; fat 6g ; fiber 1g ;

Dilly Salmon

Preparation time: 10min / **Grill time:** 15min / **Servings:** 10
Ingredients:
- 1 cup Dijon mustard
- 2/3 cup white wine or chicken broth
- 1/2 cup packed brown sugar
- 1/4 cup cider vinegar
- 3 tablespoons soy sauce
- 1 cup vegetable oil
- 1/2 cup minced fresh dill
- 1 teaspoon pepper
- 1 salmon fillet (1 inch thick and 3 pounds), cut in half widthwise

Directions:
-In a small bowl, whisk the mustard, wine, brown sugar, vinegar and soy sauce until well blended. Gradually whisk in oil. Stir in dill and pepper. Place salmon in a shallow glass dish. Pour 2 cups marinade over salmon. Cover and refrigerate for 1 hour. Cover and refrigerate remaining marinade for basting.
-Drain and discard marinade. Using long-handled tongs, moisten a paper towel with cooking oil and lightly coat the grill rack. Place salmon skin side down on grill. Grill, covered, over medium-hot heat or broil 4 in. from the heat for 5 minutes. Baste with some of the reserved marinade. Grill or broil 7-9 minutes longer or until fish flakes easily with a fork, basting occasionally.

Nutrition:calories 292kcal ;protein 19g ;carbs 7g ; fat 3g ;

Herb and Lemon Roasted Chicken

Preparation time: 30min / **Cooking time:** 1h/ **Servings:** 4

Ingredients:
-   2 tablespoons unsalted butter, softened
-   5 garlic cloves, 1 minced
-   1/2 teaspoon minced rosemary plus 2 rosemary sprigs
-   1/2 teaspoon minced thyme plus 2 thyme sprigs
-   1/2 teaspoon finely grated lemon zest
-   Salt and freshly ground pepper
-   One 4-pound chicken, at room temperature
-   1 large onion, cut into 8 wedges
-   1 lemon, cut crosswise into 8 rounds
-   1/2 cup chicken stock or low-sodium broth

Directions:
-Preheat the oven to 425° and position a rack in the lower third of the oven. In a bowl, mix the butter with the minced garlic, minced herbs and the lemon zest and season with salt and pepper.
-Pat the chicken dry. Rub half of the herb butter under the skin and the rest over the chicken; season with salt and pepper.
-Set the chicken breast-side-up on a rack in a roasting pan. Scatter the onion, lemon, garlic cloves and herb sprigs and add 1/2 cup of water. Roast for 30 minutes, until the breast is firm and just beginning to brown in spots. Using tongs, turn the chicken breast-down and roast for 20 minutes longer, until the skin is lightly browned.
-Using tongs, turn the chicken breast-side-up. Add another 1/2 cup of water. Roast for about 20 minutes longer, until an instant-read thermometer inserted in the inner thigh registers 175° to 180°.
-Tilt the chicken to drain the cavity juices into the pan; transfer the bird to a cutting board. Remove the rack from the pan and spoon off the fat. Set the pan over high heat. Add the stock and cook, scraping up any browned bits. Press the lemon to release the juices. Carve the chicken and pass the chunky jus at the table.

Nutrition: calories 510kcal ;protein 71g ;carbs 4g ; fat 31g ;

Baked Penne with Roasted Vegetables

Preparation time: 25min / **Cooking time:** 40min / **Servings:** 6
Ingredients:
- 2 red peppers, cored and cut into 2cm wide strips
- 2 courgettes, quartered lengthwise and cut into 2cm cubes
- 2 summer squash, quartered lengthwise and cut into 2cm cubes
- 4 button mushrooms, halved
- 1 yellow onion, peeled and sliced into 2cm strips
- 4 tbsp extra-virgin olive oil
- 1 tsp salt, divided
- 1 tsp freshly ground black pepper, divided
- 1 tbsp. dried Italian herb mix or herbs de Provence
- 500g penne pasta
- 120g grated fontina cheese
- 750ml marinara sauce (store bought or homemade)
- 60g grated smoked mozzarella
- 220g frozen peas, thawed
- 30g grated Parmesan, plus 30g for topping
- 30g butter, cut into small pieces

Directions:
-Preheat the oven to 220°C/gas mark8.

-On a baking sheet, toss the peppers, courgettes, squash, mushrooms, and onions with olive oil, 1/2 teaspoon salt, 1/2 teaspoon pepper, and dried herbs. Roast until tender, about 15 minutes.

-Meanwhile, bring a large pot of salted water to a boil over high heat. Add the pasta and cook for about 6 minutes. Since you will be cooking the pasta a second time in the oven, you want to make sure the inside is still hard. Drain in a colander.

-In a large bowl, toss the drained pasta with the roasted vegetables, marinara sauce, cheeses, peas, 1/2 teaspoon salt, and 1/2 teaspoon pepper. Using a wooden spoon, gently mix, until all the pasta is coated with the sauce and the ingredients are combined.

-Pour the pasta into a greased 23-cm by 33-cm pan. Top with the remaining 30g Parmesan and butter pieces. Bake until top is golden and cheese melts, about 25 minutes.

Nutrition: calories 627kcal ;protein 24g ;carbs 54g ; fat 35g ; fiber 7g ;

Hearty Chicken and Vegetable Soup

Preparation time: 15min / **Cooking time:** 45min / **Servings:** 6
Ingredients:
- 1 Stick Prairie Farms Salted Butter
- 1/2 Cup All-Purpose Flour
- 1 Qt Chicken Stock
- 1 Tsp Salt
- 1 Lb Chicken Breast Cubed
- 1 Onion Diced
- 1 Cup Potatoes Diced
- 6 Cups Water
- 1 Cup Carrots Diced
- 1 Cup Celery Diced
- 1 Can Black Eyed Peas
- 1 Can Whole Tomatoes
- Fresh Parsley Flakes

Directions:
-In large saucepan melt 1 stick of butter. Add 1/2 cup flour. Add chicken stock, and whisk until smooth.
-Add chicken, potatoes and onion in a saucepan and cook until chicken is no longer pink.
-Add water, carrots, celery and black eyed peas. Cook for 20 minutes.
-Cook until vegetables are tender.
-Garnish with fresh parsley flakes.

Nutrition:calories 284kcal ;protein 21g ;carbs 24g ; fat 12g ; fiber 3g ;

Pesto Pasta with Chicken and Tomatoes

Preparation time: 15min / **Cooking time:** 15min / **Servings:** 6
Ingredients:

Pesto:
- 1 cup firmly packed fresh basil leaves
- 1/3 cup grated Parmesan cheese
- ¼ cup olive oil
- 1 clove garlic
- 2 tablespoons sliced almonds, toasted

Pasta:
- -12 oz uncooked penne pasta (3 1/2 cups) (from 16-oz package)
- 3 cups Progresso™ chicken broth (from 32-oz carton)
- 2 cups shredded cooked chicken
- 2 cups halved cherry tomatoes
- ¼ cup julienned fresh basil leaves
- 3 tablespoons grated Parmesan cheese

Directions:

-In blender or food processor, place Pesto ingredients.

-Cover and process on medium speed about 3 minutes, stopping occasionally to scrape down sides with rubber spatula, until smooth. Set aside.

-In 4-quart saucepan, heat penne and broth just to boiling over high heat. Reduce heat to medium; cover and cook 8 to 10 minutes, stirring frequently, until al dente and liquid is almost absorbed. Remove from heat. Add pesto; stir in chicken and tomatoes; cook over medium 2 to 3 minutes or until thoroughly heated.

-Garnish with basil and 3 tablespoons Parmesan cheese.

Nutrition:calories 480kcal ;protein 27g ;carbs 52g ; fat 19g ;

Flank Steak Spinach Salad

Preparation time: 15min / **Cooking time:** 15min / **Servings:**16
Ingredients:
- 4 beef flank steaks (about 1 pound each)
- 1 bottle (16 ounces) Italian salad dressing, divided
- 1-1/4 cups uncooked wild rice
- 2 packages (6 ounces each) fresh baby spinach
- 1/2 pound fresh mushrooms, sliced
- 1 large red onion, thinly sliced
- 1 pint grape tomatoes, halved
- 1 package (2-1/2 ounces) slivered almonds, toasted

Directions:
-Place steaks in a shallow dish; add 3/4 cup salad dressing and turn to coat. Cover and refrigerate overnight. Prepare the rice according to package directions. In a bowl, combine rice with 1/2 cup salad dressing. Cover and refrigerate overnight.

-Drain steaks, discarding marinade. Grill steaks, uncovered, over medium heat for 6-8 minutes on each side or until meat reaches desired doneness (for medium-rare, a thermometer should read 135°; medium, 140°; medium-well, 145°). Let stand for 10 minutes. Thinly slice against the grain; cool to room temperature.

-To serve, arrange spinach on a large platter. Top with the rice, mushrooms, onion, tomatoes and steak. Sprinkle with almonds; drizzle with remaining salad dressing.

Nutrition:calories 305kcal ;protein 26g ;carbs 15g ; fat 15g ; fiber 2g ;

Oven-Poached Lemon Butter Cod

Preparation time: 10min / **Cooking time:** 20min / **Servings:** 6
Ingredients:
- 6 5-ounce pieces of cod, about 2 lbs
- 1/4 pound butter
- 1 small or ½ large lemon
- 1/2 cup dry vermouth
- 1 clove garlic, minced
- 1 tablespoon minced parsley
- ½ teaspoon salt
- ¼ teaspoon pepper
- Optional: extra lemon slices for garnish

Directions:
-Preheat the oven to 400 degrees. Spray a 9 x 9 pan with nonstick spray then arrange cod pieces inside of it.
-Melt butter in a small saucepan (or microwave in a bowl) then squeeze in the lemon juice. Add the vermouth, chopped parsley, garlic, salt, and -pepper to the butter mixture and mix until combined.
-Pour the butter mixture over the cod fillets
-Bake until the cod is opaque and flakes easily with a fork, approximately 15-20 minutes.
-Drizzle with butter to serve, and top with a lemon wedge if desired.

Nutrition:calories 328kcal ;protein 35g ;carbs 3g ; fat 5g ;

Easy White Wine Garlic Mussels

Preparation time: 15min / **Cooking time:** 10min / **Servings:** 4
Ingredients:
- 1½ kg (3lbs) mussels in shells / half-shell (cleaned)
- ½ cup butter
- 6 garlic cloves thinly sliced
- 1 red chilli finely chopped
- 1½ cups white wine
- juice of 1 lemon
- 2 tbsp parsley finely chopped
- salt and pepper to taste

Directions:
-Melt the butter in a deep pan with a lid.
-Add the garlic and chilli and cook for 30 seconds or until fragrant.
-Pour in the wine and lemon juice and bring to a simmer.
-Add the mussels then cover with a lid and cook for 5 minutes or until they are all open. Discard any mussels that don't open (if using whole mussels)
-Add parsley and season to taste with salt and pepper.
-Serve with crusty bread for dipping.

Nutrition:calories 524kcal ;protein 46g ;carbs 23g ; fat 18g ; fiber 3g ;

Portobello Mushroom Pizzas with Arugula Salad

Preparation time: 30min / **Cooking time:** 15min / **Servings:** 4
Ingredients:
- 8 large portobello mushroom caps (about 4 oz. each), gills removed (see Tip)
- 2 tablespoons olive oil plus 1 tsp., divided
- ½ teaspoon ground pepper, divided
- ½ cup pizza or tomato sauce
- 2 cups lightly packed baby spinach, chopped
- ½ cup sun-dried tomatoes (about 8), chopped
- 1 (14 ounce) can artichoke hearts, rinsed and chopped
- ½ cup shredded part-skim mozzarella cheese
- ¼ cup crumbled feta cheese
- ½ teaspoon dried Italian seasoning
- 1 tablespoon lemon juice
- 2 cups lightly packed baby arugula
- ¼ cup fresh basil leaves, thinly sliced

Directions:
-Preheat oven to 400 degrees F. Line a large baking sheet with foil and set a wire rack on it. Brush tops of portobello caps with 1 Tbsp. oil and place them, undersides-up, on the rack. Roast for 10 minutes. Flip and roast for 5 minutes more.
-Remove the portobellos from the oven and carefully flip them back over so that the undersides are up. Season with 1/4 tsp. pepper. Spread 1 Tbsp. sauce inside each cap. Divide spinach, sun-dried tomatoes, artichokes, mozzarella, and feta among the caps. Sprinkle with Italian seasoning. Return the portobellos to the oven and bake until the cheese is melted and starting to brown, 10 to 15 minutes.
-Meanwhile, whisk the remaining 1 Tbsp. plus 1 tsp. oil, the remaining 1/8 tsp. pepper, and lemon juice in a medium bowl. Add arugula and toss to coat.
-Garnish the portobello pizzas with basil and serve with the arugula salad.

Nutrition: calories 246kcal ;protein 14g ;carbs 25g ; fat 4g ; fiber 7g ;

Slow-Cooker Quinoa with Arugula

Preparation time: 15min / **Cooking time:** 3h / **Servings:** 6
Ingredients:
- 2 ¼ cups unsalted vegetable stock
- 1 ½ cups uncooked quinoa, rinsed
- 1 cup sliced red onions (from 1 onion)
- 2 garlic cloves, minced (about 2 teaspoons)
- 1 (15.5 ounce) can no-salt-added chickpeas (garbanzo beans), drained and rinsed
- 2 ½ tablespoons olive oil
- ¾ teaspoon kosher salt
- 2 teaspoons fresh lemon juice (from one lemon)
- ½ cup drained, chopped roasted red bell peppers (from jar)
- 4 cups baby arugula (about 4 ounces)
- 2 ounces feta cheese, crumbled (about 1/2 cup)
- 12 pitted kalamata olives, halved lengthwise
- 2 tablespoons coarsely chopped fresh oregano

Directions:
-Stir together the stock, quinoa, onions, garlic, chickpeas, 1 1/2 teaspoons of the olive oil, and 1/2 teaspoon of the salt in a 5- to 6-quart slow cooker. Cover and cook on LOW until the quinoa is tender and the stock is absorbed, 3 to 4 hours.
-Turn off the slow cooker. Fluff the quinoa mixture with a fork. Whisk together the lemon juice and remaining 2 tablespoons olive oil and 1/4 teaspoon salt. Add the olive oil mixture and red bell peppers to the slow cooker; toss gently to combine. Gently fold in the arugula. Cover and let stand until the arugula is slightly wilted, about 10 minutes. Sprinkle each serving evenly with the feta cheese, olives, and oregano.

Nutrition:calories 352kcal ;protein 12g ;carbs 46g ; fat 7g ; fiber 13g ;

Walnut Rosemary Crusted Salmon

Preparation time: 10min / **Cooking time:** 10min / **Servings:** 4
Ingredients:
- 2 teaspoons Dijon mustard
- 1 clove garlic, minced
- ¼ teaspoon lemon zest
- 1 teaspoon lemon juice
- 1 teaspoon chopped fresh rosemary
- ½ teaspoon honey
- ½ teaspoon kosher salt
- ¼ teaspoon crushed red pepper
- 3 tablespoons panko breadcrumbs
- 3 tablespoons finely chopped walnuts
- 1 teaspoon extra-virgin olive oil
- 1 (1 pound) skinless salmon fillet, fresh or frozen
- Olive oil cooking spray
- Chopped fresh parsley and lemon wedges for garnish

Directions:
-Preheat oven to 425 degrees F. Line a large rimmed baking sheet with parchment paper.
-Combine mustard, garlic, lemon zest, lemon juice, rosemary, honey, salt and crushed red pepper in a small bowl. Combine panko, walnuts and oil in another small bowl.
-Place salmon on the prepared baking sheet. Spread the mustard mixture over the fish and sprinkle with the panko mixture, pressing to adhere. Lightly coat with cooking spray.
-Bake until the fish flakes easily with a fork, about 8 to 12 minutes, depending on thickness.
-Sprinkle with parsley and serve with lemon wedges, if desired.

Nutrition:calories 222kcal ;protein 24g ;carbs 4g ; fat 12g ;

Cheesy Spinach & Artichoke Stuffed Spaghetti Squash

Preparation time: 25min / **Cooking time:** 0min / **Servings:** 4
Ingredients:
- 1 (2 1/2 to 3 pound) spaghetti squash, cut in half lengthwise and seeds removed
- 3 tablespoons water, divided
- 1 (5 ounce) package baby spinach
- 1 (10 ounce) package frozen artichoke hearts, thawed and chopped
- 4 ounces reduced-fat cream cheese, cubed and softened
- ½ cup grated Parmesan cheese, divided
- ¼ teaspoon salt
- ¼ teaspoon ground pepper
- Crushed red pepper & chopped fresh basil for garnish

Directions:
-Place squash cut-side down in a microwave-safe dish; add 2 tablespoons water. Microwave, uncovered, on High until tender, 10 to 15 minutes. (Alternatively, place squash halves cut-side down on a rimmed baking sheet. Bake at 400 degrees F until tender, 40 to 50 minutes.)
-Meanwhile, combine spinach and the remaining 1 tablespoon water in a large skillet over medium heat. Cook, stirring occasionally, until wilted, 3 to 5 minutes. Drain and transfer to a large bowl.
-Position rack in upper third of oven; preheat broiler.
-Use a fork to scrape the squash from the shells into the bowl. Place the shells on a baking sheet. Stir artichoke hearts, cream cheese, 1/4 cup Parmesan, salt and pepper into the squash mixture. Divide it between the squash shells and top with the remaining 1/4 cup Parmesan. Broil until the cheese is golden brown, about 3 minutes. Sprinkle with crushed red pepper and basil, if desired.

Nutrition:calories 223kcal ;protein 10g ;carbs 23g ; fat 10g ; fiber 9g ;

Stuffed Chicken Breasts

Preparation time: 25min / **Cooking time:** 35min / **Servings:** 8
Ingredients:
- ½ cup crumbled feta cheese
- ½ cup chopped roasted red bell peppers
- ½ cup chopped fresh spinach
- ¼ cup Kalamata olives, pitted and quartered
- 1 tablespoon chopped fresh basi
- 1 tablespoon chopped fresh flat-leaf parsley
- 2 cloves garlic, minced
- 4 (8 ounce) boneless, skinless chicken breasts
- ¼ teaspoon salt
- ½ teaspoon ground pepper
- 1 tablespoon extra-virgin olive oil
- 1 tablespoon lemon juice

Directions:
-Preheat oven to 400 degrees F. Combine feta, roasted red peppers, spinach, olives, basil, parsley and garlic in a medium bowl.
-Using a small knife, cut a horizontal slit through the thickest portion of each chicken breast to form a pocket. Stuff each breast pocket with about 1/3 cup of the feta mixture; secure the pockets using wooden picks. Sprinkle the chicken evenly with salt and pepper.
-Heat oil in a large oven-safe skillet over medium-high heat. Arrange the stuffed breasts, top-sides down, in the pan; cook until golden, about 2 minutes. Carefully flip the chicken; transfer the pan to the oven. Bake until an instant-read thermometer inserted in the thickest portion of the chicken registers 165 degrees F, 20 to 25 minutes. Drizzle the chicken evenly with lemon juice. Remove the wooden picks from the chicken before serving.

Nutrition:calories 180kcal ;protein 25g ;carbs 2g ; fat 7g ;

Charred Shrimp, Pesto & Quinoa Bowls

Preparation time: 25min / **Cooking time:** 0min / **Servings:** 4
Ingredients:
- ⅓ cup prepared pesto
- 2 tablespoons balsamic vinegar
- 1 tablespoon extra-virgin olive oi
- ½ teaspoon salt
- ¼ teaspoon ground pepper
- 1 pound peeled and deveined large shrimp (16-20 count), patted dry
- 4 cups arugula
- 2 cups cooked quinoa
- 1 cup halved cherry tomatoes
- 1 avocado, diced

Directions:
-Whisk pesto, vinegar, oil, salt and pepper in a large bowl. Remove 4 tablespoons of the mixture to a small bowl; set both bowls aside.
-Heat a large cast-iron skillet over medium-high heat. Add shrimp and cook, stirring, until just cooked through with a slight char, 4 to 5 minutes. Remove to a plate.
-Add arugula and quinoa to the large bowl with the vinaigrette and toss to coat. Divide the arugula mixture between 4 bowls. Top with tomatoes, avocado and shrimp. Drizzle each bowl with 1 tablespoon of the reserved pesto mixture.

Nutrition:calories 429kcal ;protein 30g ;carbs 29g ; fat 22g ; fiber 7g ;

Ravioli with Artichokes & Olives

Preparation time: 10min / **Cooking time:** 15min / **Servings:** 2
Ingredients:
- 2 (8 ounce) packages frozen or refrigerated spinach-and-ricotta ravioli
- ½ cup oil-packed sun-dried tomatoes, drained (2 tablespoons oil reserved)
- 1 (10 ounce) package frozen quartered artichoke hearts, thawed
- 1 (15 ounce) can no-salt-added cannellini beans, rinsed
- ¼ cup Kalamata olives, sliced
- 3 tablespoons toasted pine nuts
- ¼ cup chopped fresh basil

Directions:
-Bring a large pot of water to a boil. Cook ravioli according to package directions. Drain and toss with 1 tablespoon reserved oil; set aside.
-Heat the remaining 1 tablespoon oil in a large nonstick skillet over medium heat. Add artichokes and beans; sauté until heated through, 2 to 3 minutes.
-Fold in the cooked ravioli, sun-dried tomatoes, olives, pine nuts and basil.

Nutrition:calories 454kcal ;protein 15g ;carbs 40g ; fat 19g ; fiber 13g ;

Vegan Lentil Soup

Preparation time: 20min / **Cooking time:** 40min / **Servings:** 6
Ingredients:
- 2 tablespoons extra-virgin olive oil
- 1 ½ cups chopped yellow onions
- 1 cup chopped carrots
- 3 cloves garlic, minced
- 2 tablespoons no-salt-added tomato paste
- 4 cups reduced-sodium vegetable broth
- 1 cup water
- 1 (15 ounce) can no-salt-added cannellini beans, rinsed
- 1 cup mixed dry lentils (brown, green and black)
- ½ cup chopped sun-dried tomatoes in oil, drained
- ¾ teaspoon salt
- ½ teaspoon ground pepper
- 1 tablespoon chopped fresh dill, plus more for garnish
- 1 ½ teaspoons red-wine vinegar

Directions:
-Heat oil in a large heavy pot over medium heat. Add onions and carrots; cook, stirring occasionally, until softened, 3 to 4 minutes. Add garlic and cook, stirring constantly, until fragrant, about 1 minute. Add tomato paste and cook, stirring constantly, until the mixture is evenly coated, about 1 minute.
-Stir in broth, water, cannellini beans, lentils, sun-dried tomatoes, salt and pepper. Bring to a boil over medium-high heat; reduce heat to medium-low to maintain a simmer. Cover and simmer until the lentils are tender, 30 to 40 minutes.
-Remove from heat and stir in dill and vinegar. Garnish with additional dill, if desired and serve.

Nutrition: calories 272kcal ;protein 13g ;carbs 72g ; fat 7g ; fiber 9g ;

Green Shakshuka with Spinach, Chard & Feta

Preparation time: 30min / **Cooking time:** 0min / **Servings:** 6

Ingredients:
- ⅓ cup extra-virgin olive oil
- 1 large onion, finely chopped
- 12 ounces chard, stemmed and chopped
- 12 ounces mature spinach, stemmed and chopped
- ½ cup dry white wine
- 1 small jalapeño or serrano pepper, thinly sliced
- 2 medium cloves garlic, very thinly sliced
- ¼ teaspoon kosher salt
- ¼ teaspoon ground pepper
- ½ cup low-sodium no-chicken or chicken broth
- 2 tablespoons unsalted butter
- 6 large eggs
- ½ cup crumbled feta or goat cheese

Directions:
-Heat oil in a large skillet over medium heat. Add onion and cook, stirring often, until soft and translucent but not browned, 7 to 8 minutes. Add chard and spinach, a few handfuls at a time, and cook, stirring often, until wilted, about 5 minutes. Add wine, jalapeño (or serrano), garlic, salt and pepper; cook, stirring occasionally, until the wine is absorbed and the garlic softens, 2 to 4 minutes. Add broth and butter; cook, stirring, until the butter is melted and some of the liquid is absorbed, 1 to 2 minutes.
-Crack eggs over the vegetables. Cover and cook over medium-low heat until the whites are set, 3 to 5 minutes. Remove from heat and sprinkle with cheese; cover and let stand for 2 minutes before serving.

Nutrition:calories 296kcal ;protein 10g ;carbs 8g ; fat 23g ; fiber 3g ;

Caprese Stuffed Portobello Mushrooms

Preparation time: 25min / **Cooking time:** 15min / **Servings:** 4
Ingredients:
- 3 tablespoons extra-virgin olive oil, divided
- 1 medium clove garlic, minced
- ½ teaspoon salt, divided
- ½ teaspoon ground pepper, divided
- 4 portobello mushrooms (about 14 ounces), stems and gills removed (see Tip)
- 1 cup halved cherry tomatoes
- ½ cup fresh mozzarella pearls, drained and patted dry
- ½ cup thinly sliced fresh basil
- 2 teaspoons best-quality balsamic vinegar

Directions:
-Preheat oven to 400 degrees F.
-Combine 2 tablespoons oil, garlic, 1/4 teaspoon salt and 1/4 teaspoon pepper in a small bowl. Using a silicone brush, coat mushrooms all over with the oil mixture. Place on a large rimmed baking sheet and bake until the mushrooms are mostly soft, about 10 minutes.
-Meanwhile, stir tomatoes, mozzarella, basil and the remaining 1/4 teaspoon salt, 1/4 teaspoon pepper and 1 tablespoon oil together in a medium bowl. Once the mushrooms have softened, remove from the oven and fill with the tomato mixture. Bake until the cheese is fully melted and the tomatoes have wilted, about 12 to 15 minutes more. Drizzle each mushroom with 1/2 teaspoon vinegar and serve.

Nutrition: calories 189kcal ;protein 6g ;carbs 6g ; fat 16g ; fiber 2g ;

Roasted Salmon with Wild Rice Pilaf

Preparation time: 15min / **Cooking time:** 15min / **Servings:** 4
Ingredients:
- 5 skinless salmon fillets, fresh or frozen (1 1/4 lbs.)
- 2 tablespoons balsamic vinegar
- 1 tablespoon honey
- ¼ teaspoon salt
- ⅛ teaspoon ground pepper
- 1 cup chopped red and/or yellow bell pepper
- ½ to 1 small jalapeño pepper, seeded and finely chopped
- 2 scallions (green parts only), thinly sliced
- ¼ cup chopped fresh Italian parsley
- 2 2/3 cups Wild Rice Pilaf (see Associated Recipes)

Directions:
-Thaw salmon, if frozen. Preheat oven to 425 degrees F. Line a 15-by-10-inch baking pan with parchment paper. Place the salmon in the prepared pan. Whisk vinegar and honey in a small bowl; drizzle half of the mixture over the salmon. Sprinkle with salt and pepper.
-Roast the salmon until the thickest part flakes easily, about 15 minutes. Drizzle with the remaining vinegar mixture.
-Coat a 10-inch nonstick skillet with cooking spray; heat over medium heat. Add bell pepper and jalapeño; cook, stirring frequently, just until tender, 3 to 5 minutes. Remove from heat. Stir in scallion greens.
-Top 4 of the salmon fillets with the pepper mixture and parsley. Serve with pilaf. (Refrigerate the remaining salmon for another use, see Note.)
Nutrition:calories 339kcal ;protein 29g ;carbs 42g ; fat 5g ; fiber 3g ;

Herby Fish with Wilted Greens & Mushrooms

Preparation time: 25min / **Cooking time:** 0min / **Servings:** 4
Ingredients:
- 3 tablespoons olive oil, divided
- ½ large sweet onion, sliced
- 3 cups sliced cremini mushrooms
- 2 cloves garlic, sliced
- 4 cups chopped kale
- 1 medium tomato, diced
- 2 teaspoons Mediterranean Herb Mix (see Associated Recipes), divided
- 1 tablespoon lemon juice
- ½ teaspoon salt, divided
- ½ teaspoon ground pepper, divided
- 4 (4 ounce) cod, sole, or tilapia fillets
- Chopped fresh parsley, for garnish

Directions:

-Heat 1 Tbsp. oil in a large saucepan over medium heat. Add onion; cook, stirring occasionally, until translucent, 3 to 4 minutes. Add mushrooms and garlic; cook, stirring occasionally, until the mushrooms release their liquid and begin to brown, 4 to 6 minutes. Add kale, tomato, and 1 tsp. herb mix. Cook, stirring occasionally, until the kale is wilted and the mushrooms are tender, 5 to 7 minutes. Stir in lemon juice and 1/4 tsp. each salt and pepper. Remove from heat, cover, and keep warm.

-Sprinkle fish with the remaining 1 tsp. herb mix and 1/4 tsp. each salt and pepper. Heat the remaining 2 Tbsp. oil in a large nonstick skillet over medium-high heat. Add the fish and cook until the flesh is opaque, 2 to 4 minutes per side, depending on thickness. Transfer the fish to 4 plates or a serving platter. Top and surround the fish with the vegetables; sprinkle with parsley, if desired.

Nutrition:calories 220kcal ;protein 18g ;carbs 11g ; fat 11g ; fiber 3g ;

Chicken with Tomato-Balsamic Pan Sauce

Preparation time: 35min / **Cooking time:** 0min / **Servings:** 4
Ingredients:
- 2 8-ounce boneless, skinless chicken breasts
- ½ teaspoon salt, divided
- ½ teaspoon ground pepper, divided
- ¼ cup white whole-wheat flour
- 3 tablespoons extra-virgin olive oil, divided
- ½ cup halved cherry tomatoes
- 2 tablespoons sliced shallot
- ¼ cup balsamic vinegar
- 1 cup low-sodium chicken broth
- 1 tablespoon minced garlic
- 1 tablespoon fennel seeds, toasted and lightly crushed
- 1 tablespoon butter

Directions:
-Remove and reserve chicken tenders (if attached) for another use. Slice each breast in half horizontally to make 4 pieces total. Place on a cutting board and cover with a large piece of plastic wrap. Pound with the smooth side of a meat mallet or a heavy saucepan to an even thickness of about 1/4 inch. Sprinkle with 1/4 teaspoon each salt and pepper. Place flour in a shallow dish and dredge the cutlets to coat both sides, shaking off excess. (Discard remaining flour.)
-Heat 2 tablespoons oil in a large skillet over medium-high heat. Add 2 pieces of chicken and cook, turning once, until evenly browned and cooked through, 2 to 3 minutes per side. Transfer to a large serving plate and tent with foil to keep warm. Repeat with the remaining chicken.
-Add the remaining 1 tablespoon oil, tomatoes and shallot to the pan. Cook, stirring occasionally, until softened, 1 to 2 minutes. Add vinegar; bring to a boil. Cook, scraping up any browned bits from the bottom of the pan, until the vinegar is reduced by about half, about 45 seconds. Add broth, garlic, fennel seeds and the remaining 1/4 teaspoon salt and pepper. Cook, stirring, until the sauce is reduced by about half, 4 to 7 minutes. Remove from heat; stir in butter. Serve the sauce over the chicken.

Nutrition: calories 295kcal ;protein 25g ;carbs 15g ; fat 16g ; fiber 3g ;

Roasted Pistachio-Crusted Salmon with Broccoli

Preparation time: 30min / **Cooking time:** 15min / **Servings:** 4

Ingredients:
- 8 cups broccoli florets with 2-inch stalks attached
- 2 cloves garlic, slice
- 3 tablespoons extra-virgin olive oil, divided
- ¾ teaspoon salt, divided
- ½ teaspoon ground pepper, divided
- ½ cup salted pistachios, coarsely chopped
- 2 tablespoons chopped fresh chives
- Zest of 1 medium lemon, plus wedges for serving
- 4 teaspoons mayonnaise
- 1 ¼ pounds salmon fillet, cut into 4 portions

Directions:
-Preheat oven to 425 degrees F. Coat a large rimmed baking sheet with cooking spray.
-Combine broccoli, garlic, 2 tablespoons oil, 1/2 teaspoon salt and 1/4 teaspoon pepper on the prepared baking sheet. Roast for 5 minutes.
-Meanwhile, combine pistachios, chives, lemon zest, the remaining 1 tablespoon oil and 1/4 teaspoon each salt and pepper in a small bowl. Spread 1 teaspoon mayonnaise over each salmon portion and top with the pistachio mixture.
-Move the broccoli to one side of the baking sheet and place the salmon on the empty side. Roast until the salmon is opaque in the center and the broccoli is just tender, 8 to 15 minutes more, depending on thickness. Serve with lemon wedges, if desired.

Nutrition:calories 424kcal ;protein 36g ;carbs 12g ; fat g ; fiber g ;

Burgers with Herb-Feta Sauce

Preparation time: 25min / **Cooking time:** 0min / **Servings:** 4
Ingredients:
- 1 cup nonfat plain Greek yogurt
- ¼ cup crumbled feta cheese
- 3 tablespoons chopped fresh oregano, divided
- ¼ teaspoon lemon zest
- 2 teaspoons lemon juice
- ¾ teaspoon salt, divided
- 1 small red onion
- 1 pound ground lamb or ground beef
- ½ teaspoon ground pepper
- 2 whole-wheat pitas, halved, split and warmed
- 1 cup sliced cucumber
- 1 plum tomato, sliced

Directions:
-Preheat grill to medium-high or preheat broiler to high.
-Mix yogurt, feta, 1 tablespoon oregano, lemon zest, lemon juice and 1/4 teaspoon salt in a small bowl.
-Cut 1/4-inch-thick slices of onion to make 1/4 cup. Finely chop more onion to make 1/4 cup. (Reserve any remaining onion for another use.) Mix the chopped onion and meat in a large bowl with the remaining 2 tablespoons oregano and 1/2 teaspoon each salt and pepper. Form into 4 oval patties, about 4 inches by 3 inches.
-Grill or broil the burgers, turning once, until an instant-read thermometer registers 160 degrees F, 4 to 6 minutes per side. Serve in pita halves, with the sauce, onion slices, cucumber and tomato.
Nutrition:calories 375kcal ;protein 29g ;carbs 23g ; fat 18g ; fiber 2g ;

Roasted Fish with Vegetables

Preparation time: 35min / **Cooking time:** 20min / **Servings:** 4
Ingredients:
- 1 pound fingerling potatoes, halved lengthwise
- 2 tablespoons olive oil
- 5 garlic cloves, coarsely chopped
- ½ teaspoon sea salt
- ½ teaspoon freshly ground black pepper
- 4 5 to 6-ounce fresh or frozen skinless salmon fillets
- 2 medium red, yellow and/or orange sweet peppers, cut into rings
- 2 cups cherry tomatoes
- 1 ½ cups chopped fresh parsley (1 bunch)
- ¼ cup pitted kalamata olives, halved
- ¼ cup finely snipped fresh oregano or 1 Tbsp. dried oregano, crushed
- 1 lemon

Directions:
-Preheat oven to 425 degrees F. Place potatoes in a large bowl. Drizzle with 1 Tbsp. of the oil and sprinkle with garlic and 1/8 tsp. of the salt and black pepper; toss to coat. Transfer to a 15x10-inch baking pan; cover with foil. Roast 30 minutes.
-Meanwhile, thaw salmon, if frozen. Combine, in the same bowl, sweet peppers, tomatoes, parsley, olives, oregano and 1/8 tsp. of the salt and black pepper. Drizzle with remaining 1 Tbsp. oil; toss to coat.
-Rinse salmon; pat dry. Sprinkle with remaining 1/4 tsp. salt and black pepper. Spoon sweet pepper mixture over potatoes and top with salmon. Roast, uncovered, 10 minutes more or just until salmon flakes.
-Remove zest from lemon. Squeeze juice from lemon over salmon and vegetables. Sprinkle with zest.

Nutrition:calories 422kcal ;protein 32g ;carbs 31g ; fat 18g ; fiber 5g ;

Pea & Spinach Carbonara

Preparation time: 20min / **Cooking time:** 0min / **Servings:** 4

Ingredients:
- 1 ½ tablespoons extra-virgin olive oil
- ½ cup panko breadcrumbs, preferably whole-wheat
- 1 small clove garlic, minced
- 8 tablespoons grated Parmesan cheese, divided
- 3 tablespoons finely chopped fresh parsley
- 3 large egg yolks
- 1 large egg
- ½ teaspoon ground pepper
- ¼ teaspoon salt
- 1 (9 ounce) package fresh tagliatelle or linguine
- 8 cups baby spinach
- 1 cup peas (fresh or frozen)

Directions:

-Put 10 cups of water in a large pot and bring to a boil over high heat.

-Meanwhile, heat oil in a large skillet over medium-high heat. Add breadcrumbs and garlic; cook, stirring frequently, until toasted, about 2 minutes. Transfer to a small bowl and stir in 2 tablespoons Parmesan and parsley. Set aside.

-Whisk the remaining 6 tablespoons Parmesan, egg yolks, egg, pepper and salt in a medium bowl.

-Cook pasta in the boiling water, stirring occasionally, for 1 minute. Add spinach and peas and cook until the pasta is tender, about 1 minute more. Reserve 1/4 cup of the cooking water. Drain and place in a large bowl.

-Slowly whisk the reserved cooking water into the egg mixture. Gradually add the mixture to the pasta, tossing with tongs to combine. Serve topped with the reserved breadcrumb mixture.

Nutrition:calories 430kcal ;protein 20g ;carbs 54g ; fat 8g ; fiber 14g ;

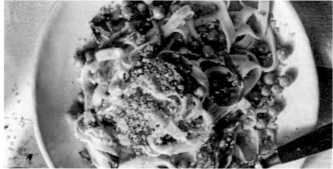

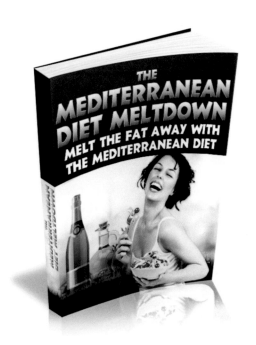

We always love to offer free books to our readers.

Don't forget to get your FREE book below.

https://bit.ly/FreeMediterranean

Milton Keynes UK
Ingram Content Group UK Ltd.
UKRC030300020424
440455UK00005B/61